Was it despiritualization that motivated the Indians to kill with such
lack of restraint they ask? Or was it
the need for pelts and skins to exchange for guns and other items—a
need growing out of their encounters
with European traders and colonists?
And to what extent can Martin's thesis
be extended to other tribes in other
parts of the North American continent—for instance, the southeastern
Indians?

Calvin Martin responds in the final
chapter of the volume. The book's appeal transcends the boundaries of anthropology and history to include
anyone interested in the Indians of
North America.

SHEPARD KRECH III, the editor of this
volume and one of the contributors, is
an associate professor of anthropology
at George Mason University.

INDIANS, ANIMALS,
AND THE FUR TRADE

INDIANS, ANIMALS,
AND THE FUR TRADE
A CRITIQUE OF
KEEPERS OF THE GAME

EDITED BY SHEPARD KRECH III

The University of Georgia Press Athens

Copyright © 1981 by
the University of Georgia Press
Athens, Georgia 30602
All rights reserved
Set in Palatino
Designed by Richard Hendel
Printed in the United States of America

Library of Congress Cataloging in Publication Data

Main entry under title:

Indians, animals, and the fur trade.

"Initial versions of these papers were presented in the symposium, 'Ethno-historical perspectives on Keepers of the game,' at the twenty-seventh annual meeting of the American Society for Ethnohistory, Albany, N.Y., October 11–14, 1979"—Introd.
Includes bibliographies and index.
1. Martin, Calvin. Keepers of the game—Addresses, essays, lectures. 2. Indians of North America—Canada—Hunting—Addresses, essays, lectures. 3. Indians of North America—Canada—Religion and mythology—Addresses, essays, lectures. 4. Micmac Indians—Hunting—Addresses, essays, lectures. 5. Chippewa Indians—Hunting—Addresses, essays, lectures. 6. Fur trade—Canada—Addresses, essays, lectures. I. Krech, Shepard, 1944–
E78.C2M3334   971.004'97   81-1351
ISBN 0-8203-0563-4   AACR2

"The War between Indians and Animals"
by Calvin Martin is reprinted with permission
from Natural History, June–July 1978.
Copyright © American Museum of Natural History, 1978.

CONTENTS

Introduction SHEPARD KRECH III   1

1. The War between Indians and Animals   11
CALVIN MARTIN

2. Ontario Native People and the Epidemics of 1634–1640   19
BRUCE G. TRIGGER

3. Northeastern Indian Concepts of Conservation and   39
the Fur Trade: A Critique of Calvin Martin's Thesis
CHARLES A. BISHOP

4. *Keepers of the Game* and the Nature of Explanation   59
DEAN R. SNOW

5. "Throwing Bad Medicine": Sorcery, Disease, and the Fur   73
Trade among the Kutchin and Other Northern Athapaskans
SHEPARD KRECH III

6. The Nature of Evil: Of Whales and Sea Otters   109
LYDIA T. BLACK

7. Why the Southeastern Indians Slaughtered Deer   155
CHARLES M. HUDSON, JR.

8. Animals and Disease in Indian Belief   177
WILLIAM C. STURTEVANT

9. Comment CALVIN MARTIN   189

Contributors 199   Index 203

INTRODUCTION

SHEPARD KRECH III

ANTHROPOLOGISTS, HISTORIANS, and other scholars have had a long-standing interest in analyses and interpretations of North American Indian participation in the fur trade. The papers in this volume continue in this tradition, but the authors—all of whom are both anthropologists and ethnohistorians—address specifically a challenge presented by Calvin Martin, a historian, with the 1978 publication of *Keepers of the Game: Indian-Animal Relationships and the Fur Trade*.[1]

In *Keepers of the Game* (1978a, cited hereafter by page numbers only) and elsewhere (1978b), Martin proposes a novel thesis to account for the enthusiastic participation of some Subarctic Indians in the fur trade. Martin sets out to resolve what he terms an anomaly: Indians were almost everywhere "the principal agent[s] in the over-hunting of fur-bearers" that culminated in "the destruction of fur and game resources"; yet, among aboriginal eastern Subarctic Indian groups, "the single most important deterrent to excessive hunting . . . was the fear of spiritual reprisal for indiscreet slaughter." Hunting was a "holy occupation," and "compelling sanctions against overkilling wildlife" included the belief that the spirit of an offended animal "could inflict sickness." Prior to the advent of Europeans and their diseases, the sickness sanction, the "threat of retaliation . . . had the probable effect of placing an upper limit on the number of animals slain" (pp. 2–3, 18, 39, 113).

Why, then, did the Indians participate with such gusto in the fur trade? Martin rejects conventional economic explanations that focus on Indian desire for European trade goods as inadequate and incomplete: "No doubt [acquisitive feelings] were there," Martin (p. 19) writes, but these feelings came later on.

What preceded acquisitive feelings were epidemic diseases of

3

European origin, and turning in depth to the eastern Algonkian Micmac, Martin argues that these diseases, which in some instances may have antedated the actual sighting of Europeans, decimated the Micmac, and that Micmac shamans "frequently diagnosed" illness as due to the violation of a taboo associated with animals. Taboo violation risked offending an animal spirit, which then might retaliate and either adversely affect hunting success, cause game to be scarce, or "inflict sickness" (pp. 38–39).

Epidemics, in addition to inflicting mortality, produced "despiritualization" (p. 113): they "rendered the Indian's (particularly the shaman's) ability to control and otherwise influence the supernatural realm dysfunctional—because his magic and other traditional cures were now ineffective—thereby causing him to apostatize (in effect); this in turn subverted the 'retaliation' principle of taboo and opened the way to a corruption of the Indian-land relationship which soon gathered momentum under the influence of the fur trade" (p. 53).

Martin argues that "it is not unreasonable to assume" that the Micmac blamed animals for diseases and "repudiated his role within the ecosystem. . . . Lured by European commodities, equipped with European technology, urged by European traders, deprived of a sense of responsibility and accountability for the land and no longer inhibited by taboo, the Micmac began to overkill systematically those wildlife which had now become so profitable and even indispensable to his new way of life" (pp. 54, 61–62). Martin concludes that his is a "novel interpretation of the fur trade—from the Indian side of the issue" (p. 154). Political or economic aspects of the trade may have become important, but "slightly antedating this was the timely rationalization for wantonly slaughtering such unprecedented numbers of game. Man and animal were at war, and the rules of the usually amicable but guarded relationship were altered accordingly" (p. 154).

Reactions to Martin's ideas have appeared to date mainly in reviews and have been mixed. Barbara Graymont regards *Keepers of the Game* as a "brilliant study of the Indian fur trade . . .

4

a hypothesis that is backed up by a breath-taking amount of skilled interdisciplinary research and also one that attempts, with great success, to present the case from the Indian point of view" (1979:537–38). Others are not nearly so positive. John Ewers suggests that Martin's arguments "are based as much on analogy and speculation as upon the historical and ethnological literature" (1979:378). Cornelius Jaenen sees problems with "causal patterns, the sequence of events, and the placement of key quotations in their precise historical contexts" (1979:318–19). Leonard Carlson considers "the neglect of economic factors" to be unconvincing (1978:1026).

Specific assessments aside, an almost unanimous opinion is that *Keepers of the Game* is important—"original" and "provocative" describe the reaction to this book, the 1979 recipient of the Albert J. Beveridge Award of the American Historical Association. In 1978, Francis Jennings (Ms.) commented: "This is a book to start arguments rather than one to settle them. As such, it has a proper place in the literature, and may we all learn from it to work more sensitively on the issues it has raised."

This collection of essays is published in the spirit of sensitive work on the issues Martin has raised. These issues—Martin's thesis—he develops most fully for the eastern Subarctic Micmac and Ojibwa, although he would have the thesis extend to "other areas of the continent where the trade was prosecuted with comparable vigor" (p. 184). Beyond the eastern Subarctic the thesis would embrace the Chipewyan and Koyukon (mentioned on numerous occasions) and other Northern Athapaskans of the western Subarctic; "less confidently" (p. 185) the Huron, Cherokee, and other horticulturalists of the Northeast and Southeast; even the fur seal and sea otter trade (p. 186) deserves rethinking.

Martin's essay "The War between Indians and Animals" (1978b) is reprinted as Chapter 1 in this volume. The geographical focus of the next three chapters is the Northeast, the area of greatest concern to Martin.

Bruce G. Trigger, writing of the Iroquoian Huron and the Algonkian-speaking Algonkin, Montagnais, and others in "Ontario Native People and the Epidemics of 1634–1640," suggests that there is "no hard evidence of major epidemics" in southern Ontario in the sixteenth century. By the time that the first cycle of major epidemics (which led to a population reduction of roughly 50 percent) began, the Huron were already dependent on the trade, having recognized the technological superiority of some items, and had depleted some beaver stocks. Furthermore, the Huron associated disease, not with animal spirits, but with the creator, Aataentsic, or they blamed sorcerers, including some French, for illness.

In "Northeastern Indian Concepts of Conservation and the Fur Trade: A Critique of Calvin Martin's Thesis," Charles A. Bishop argues that while in some cases Indians may have blamed animals for their afflictions, this is inadequate as a general explanation for trade in the region, since the effects of disease were not constant and the French were blamed for sickness on some occasions; importantly, he suggests also that Indians were maximizing leisure, prestige, generosity, and security by participating in the trade.

Dean R. Snow, in *"Keepers of the Game* and the Nature of Explanation,"· proposes that causation is systemically complex, that ideology is rarely a major antecedent variable, and that, beyond one or two isolated instances, Martin's explanation is inadequate, especially for the Eastern Abenaki.

The authors of these three chapters agree with Martin that a goal of ethnohistorical research is to attempt to understand Indian motivation in the trade. Furthermore, they agree that exogenous epidemic diseases had a devastating impact on Indian populations. But these authors part company with Martin in their questioning both the evidence for widespread epidemics antedating the arrival of Europeans and for despiritualization; in their specifications of the exact timing of the sequence of epidemics, fur trade participation, and overkill; in arguing that it is extremely difficult to reconstruct patterns of native thought, especially in regard to disease etiology (where sorcerers or other beings make animals seem unimportant as major disease-causing agents); and in their endorsement of a materialist versus an idealist explanation in an admittedly complex system of causation of Indian participation in the trade. A materialist explanation, they argue, supports data in historical records and is sufficient to account for Indian participation in the trade.

The next three chapters, 5 through 7, examine whether or not Martin's thesis can be extended from the eastern Subarctic to other areas of the continent. In " 'Throwing Bad Medicine': Sorcery, Disease, and the Fur Trade among the Kutchin," Shepard Krech III focuses on the Northern Athapaskan Kutchin, hunter-fishers of the western Subarctic, who participated with enthusiasm in an exchange of furs for beads and guns, and who concurrently were devastated by epidemics. Contrary to Martin's propositions, however, the Kutchin exhibited commercial tendencies from the earliest days of contact, and they blamed shamans and sorcerers for sickness, disease, and death. Comparative data from the Chipewyan, Koyukon, and other groups support the opinion that Northern Athapaskans blamed sorcerers, not animals, for diseases.

In "The Nature of Evil: Of Whales and Sea Otters," Lydia T. Black demonstrates that Martin's hypothesis cannot be extended to the Aleut sea otter and fur seal trade. Sea otters were not conceptualized as disease-causing agents; furthermore, ethnohistorical records point to a clear connection between a market economy, the use of firearms (by non-Aleut hunters), and the late-nineteenth-century decline of sea otters.

Charles M. Hudson, Jr., continues the materialist assault on Martin's hypothesis in "Why the Southeastern Indians Slaughtered Deer." Although Native Americans in the Southeast did believe that animals (or sorcerers or spirits) could cause disease and although there were epidemics at an early date (sixteenth and seventeenth centuries), the available evidence makes it doubtful that animals were blamed. Hudson suggests that deer (and slaves) were hunted and exchanged for guns and other perceived needs for materialist reasons, linked ultimately to worldwide economic and political transformations.

Once again, the authors of these essays point to (1) either key animals conceptualized as unimportant disease-causing agents or other agents, such as sorcerers, of equal importance or specifically associated with epidemics in historical sources and (2) the empirical connection between killing fur-bearers and mercantilist, materialist tendencies.

Where does this leave us? With a thesis that cannot be extended to other areas of the continent? With one that may hold only for the isolated instances noticed, recorded, and alluded to in the late eighteenth century by surveyor David Thompson, trader Alexander Henry, and a few others?

William C. Sturtevant, in "Animals and Diseases in Indian Belief," wonders whether the explanation holds even for those isolated instances. Turning to the Ojibwa and the ethnography of A. Irving Hallowell, Sturtevant points out that an infraction of a taboo was likely to cause, not sickness, but a scarcity of animals and that it makes more sense to think of Ojibwa as blaming themselves, not animals, for taboo violation; there was, therefore, no reason to blame (and take revenge on) animals for the symptoms of taboo violation.

This paper, more than any other, illustrates the difficulties involved in revealing Native American religious ideas, world view, or motivations and in interpreting behavior by concepts whose meanings are not wholly appropriate. These issues have been considered in passing by the other contributors: for instance, Bishop asks why, if Indians did believe that animals were responsible for diseases, they weren't even more courteous to them; Snow argues that shamans transformed into animal forms, not animals themselves, were disease agents; Krech points out the difficulty in applying the concept of waste (or conservation) to Chipewyan caribou harvest.

In his "Comment," Calvin Martin focuses on the issues raised by Sturtevant, not on the alternative interpretations of historical documents or the materialist explanations in the other papers. Martin shows how difficult it is to rely on a single ethnographic document and how we must all, as ethnohistorians, treat these documents with as much critical acuity as we do historical sources. Martin adheres to his thesis, presented in abbreviated fashion in the first chapter, and remains "unreconstructed" after reading the papers in this volume. Whether or not he should is something that readers of this volume must judge for themselves. No matter what the eventual outcome of this debate, anthropologists and historians, as ethnohistorians, should not cease their attempts to reconstruct and reveal the world views and religious ideas of Native North American peoples and their reasons for participating in the fur trade. Calvin Martin's challenge and the responses in this volume, I hope, bring us one step closer to that goal.

Notes

1. Initial versions of these papers were presented in the symposium "Ethnohistorical Perspectives on *Keepers of the Game*" at the Twenty-seventh Annual Meeting of the American Society for Ethnohistory, Albany, N.Y., October 11–14, 1979.

References Cited

Carlson, Leonard
    1978   *Review of* Keepers of the Game. Journal of Economic History 38: 1026–27.
Ewers, John C.
    1979   *Review of* Keepers of the Game. Western Historical Quarterly 10: 376–78.

Graymont, Barbara
   1979   *Review of* Keepers of the Game. American Historical
           Review 84:537–38.
Jaenen, Cornelius
   1979   *Review of* Keepers of the Game. William and Mary
           Quarterly 36:317–20.
Jennings, Francis
   1978   Games of the Keepers: Comments on Calvin Martin,
           Keepers of the Game. Paper presented at the
           Twenty-sixth Annual Meeting of the American So-
           ciety for Ethnohistory, Austin, Texas, November
           2–4, 1978.
Martin, Calvin
   1978*a*   Keepers of the Game: Indian-Animal Relationships
            and the Fur Trade. Berkeley: University of California
            Press.
   1978*b*   The War between Indians and Animals. Natural His-
            tory 87(6):92–96.

CHAPTER ONE

THE WAR BETWEEN
INDIANS AND ANIMALS

CALVIN MARTIN

OVER THE past five centuries the American Indian has been called everything from "noble savage" to "besotted alcoholic"— epithets that say as much about the conscience of contemporary white society as they do about the state of the Indian. So it was that in the heat and froth of the 1960s environmental movement, yet another title—"ecological Indian"—was conferred on the idealized native American, who was paraded out before an admiring throng and hailed as the high priest of the Ecology Cult. According to law professor Rennard Strickland, "*It is not an accident that the idea of ecology and the ideal of the Indian should emerge simultaneously as national issues,*" and former Secretary of the Interior Stewart Udall concurred. Both Indian activist Vine Deloria, Jr., and Kiowa novelist N. Scott Momaday urged white Americans to "adopt Indian ways to survive."

Critics of the ecological Indian were quick to respond. In 1972 the frontier historian W. H. Hutchinson expressed a strongly negative opinion in his "Dissenting Voice Raised Against the Resurrection of the Myth of the Noble Savage." A past master of sarcasm and metaphor, Hutchinson blasted the dewy-eyed romantics who would claim for the Indian such a delicate ecological conscience "as to make the Sierra Club seem an association of strip miners by comparison." Nature, as he cogently put it, "is *not* a benign bovine with a teat for every questing mouth!" Hutchinson went on to say that the Indian revered nature because he had no other choice; that he perceived nature as being controlled by supernatural forces that he was obliged to propitiate if he hoped for success in life; failure to perform the proper rituals, adhere to taboos, and conduct ceremonials was tantamount to inviting disaster. We ought to dry our eyes and recognize that the Indian was above all a self-centered pragmatist when it came to land use.

Hutchinson ended his assault with a troubling question: "If the Amerind was a truly dedicated ecologist, why did he so succumb to the artifacts offered him by Europeans that he stripped his land of furs and pelts to get them?" His answer: "He did so because he was only human. The white man offered him material goods—iron and woolens and gewgaws and alcohol— which he could not resist. These riches, which is what they were, gave his life an expanded dimension it had never known before. No power on earth could keep him from getting these things by raid or trade, once he had been exposed to them. To ask him to have refrained from making his material life fuller and richer is to ask him for far more than we ever have asked of ourselves." Hutchinson had identified the ecological Indian's Achilles' heel.

Hutchinson's response is essentially that of most other ethnohistorians who have pondered the Indian's role in the fur trade—the most notorious and unequivocal case of resource abuse by native North Americans. There can be no denying that the native hunter was the principal agent of wildlife destruction in most theaters of the fur trade, particularly in Canada where whites operated mainly as brokers rather than as hunters and trappers. In Canada, where the evidence against the Indian is most damaging, there were, in fact, mitigating circumstances that make the Subarctic Indian's motive in wildlife extermination considerably less crass than scholars such as Hutchinson have conceded. Without denying the essential validity of Hutchinson's statement that Indians were initially impressed with the items proffered them by Europeans—and at the risk of being accused of ennobling the "savage" once more—I would give a somewhat different, localized version of what happened when all those marvelous items of Old World origin first reached the native hunters of eastern Canada.

Put succinctly, the fur trade throughout eastern Canada was a paradox. Native hunters felt a sense of spiritual kinship with major game animals, including those sought for their pelts—a relationship tempered by genuine awe and fear of these powerful animal beings and their spiritual wardens, or game bosses. Historic evidence seems to corroborate the modern ethnographer's claim that Subarctic Indians have traditionally been obsessed by the responsibilities of the hunter and the hunted toward one another. Included among these responsibilities has been the understanding between man and animal that game can be harvested only in modest quantities. Animals have always considered immoderate slaughter to be presumptuous. According to present-day tribesmen and their early historic ancestors, game animals voluntarily surrender themselves to be slain by the needy hunter. The injunction against overkill could not be circumvented by disposing of the animal remains in a manner pleasing to the slain beast, after which regeneration would normally occur. Such procedures worked only when the hunter restricted his take to a reasonable quota agreed upon between his spirit being and that of the animal he yearned for, and communicated with, in his dreaming, singing, drumming, and sweating—all of this prior to the actual hunt.

Subarctic hunters also considered animals to be persons with whom humans could talk and enjoy other forms of social intercourse, including the right to harvest these "animal persons" on a limited basis. In sum, man and animal have traditionally had a relationship of mutual courtesy: intelligent animal beings and intelligent human beings had contracted long ago not to abuse one another. Animals took offense not only when they were slaughtered in excessive numbers but also when they were subjected to other forms of disrespect: when humans failed to address them by the proper titles of endearment or when their remains were defiled by being thrown to the dogs or when their flesh was consumed by menstruating women. Humans, in their turn, were offended when animals refused to be taken in their traps or otherwise eluded the famished hunter and his family. Whenever one side transgressed the bounds of propriety the other side unleashed its arsenal of weapons to chastise the offenders and bring them back into line. For their part, animals could punish humans by fleeing their hunting areas, rendering their weapons impotent, or afflicting them with disease.

The paradox emerges in the early records, which describe how Canadian Indians hunted fur-bearers and other mammals with abandon. One would think that their hunting ethic would have precluded the orgiastic destruction of wildlife. But that ethic was apparently suspended during the heyday of the Canadian fur trade. The Indian described in these records is peculiarly hostile toward animals: he hunts the beaver and other large game with a vengeance; his mood is vindictive. Furthermore, he has clearly lost touch with much of the spirit world that sustained him prior to the coming of Europeans. Sometime in the early contact period, nature—the universe—seems to have become inarticulate and the dialogue between human persons and animal persons ceased, at least temporarily. The French surgeon-botanist Sieur de Dièreville conveyed in 1708 the essence of this sentiment in some wretched verse on the art of beaver hunting:

> They [the natives] take precautions in regard to all
> The varied needs of life. The Indian race,
> Well qualified to judge the point, because
> Of its familiarity with all their arts,
> Believe that they [beaver] have been endowed
> With an abounding genius, and hold too
> It is pure malice that they do not talk.

Or as the Recollet priest Chrestien Le Clercq explained it in 1691, the Micmac Indians, who still insisted that the beaver had "sense" and formed a "separate nation," maintained that they "would cease to make war upon these animals if these would speak, howsoever little, in order that they might learn whether the Beavers are among their friends or their enemies." Near the turn of the nineteenth century, surveyor David Thompson and fur trader Alexander Henry, the Elder, encountered Cree and

Ojibwa in southern Manitoba and the upper Great Lakes region who referred to some sort of conspiracy of animals against mankind for which the beaver, at any rate, were "now all to be destroyed." Together with these cryptic remarks on the overt antagonism between man and animal, there is considerable explicit and inferential evidence proving that the man-animal relationship had gone sour.

Indian hunters now tracked game remorselessly; no thought was given to the animals' welfare as the beaver and other fur-bearers were hounded to near extinction in parts of the north woods. What made the Indian apostatize? I believe the answer lies in the devastating impact of diseases on these people.

The early records contain frequent references to eastern Canadian Indians, in common with native Americans throughout the hemisphere, being decimated by a variety of Old World contagions, most significantly, smallpox, influenza, and plague. Folkloric and circumstantial evidence place the arrival of these diseases well before the date of first recorded European contact. In all likelihood coastal Indians were exposed to deadly bacteria and viruses carried by Bristol, Norman, Basque, and other European fishermen who were working the various banks off the Canadian Maritimes some years before the Genoan-born merchant John Cabot "discovered" and officially took possession of the area for the English king, Henry VII, in 1497. Transmitted by infected natives, the diseases rolled inland. And the death rate was appalling. In the early seventeenth century the Jesuit Pierre Biard recorded that the Micmacs "are astonished and often complain that . . . they are dying fast, and the population is thinning out." Similar testimonials occur throughout the *Jesuit Relations* and other early records of New France. The victims had never encountered these diseases until the Europeans arrived, and the high mortality was due to the natives' lack of adequate immunological protection.

Eastern Canadian Indians have always interpreted major illness as punishment for some sort of transgression, generally meted out by offended wildlife spirits. Fitting the ethnographic and historic records together, I conjecture that prior to sustained contact with whites, who subsequently would be correctly suspected of being responsible for this calamity, the eastern Canadian aborigine followed conventional logic and blamed these mysterious, devastating epidemics on angered wildlife. Here was the "conspiracy" of animal against man alluded to by Cree and Ojibwa sources: wildlife had decided, for some obscure reason, to direct their most potent weapon against man, who now felt himself imperiled by their terrible wrath. Wildlife had broken the compact of mutual courtesy. The dialogue between man and animal became acrimonious and then simply ended for many individuals.

Such was the emotion-charged setting that European traders and missionaries penetrated in the seventeenth and eighteenth centuries. Gently urging the Indians to furnish furs for the European market and renounce their "superstitions" for the sake of the Gospel, the Europeans could not have found a more receptive audience. The Indians were predisposed to respond positively to both requests. Their spiritual complex a shambles, they now turned on their former colleagues, the game, with a vengeance and an improved hunting technology. The Indians were, as some Micmac aptly phrased it, literally making war upon the beaver.

The Canadian Indian may well have been a conservationist of animal resources as long as he considered them articulate and congenial beings—a hunting ethic that has been revived in this century by Indians in many parts of Canada. The message for those environmentalists who have looked to the Indian for spiritual inspiration, however, is not encouraging. The northern hunter conserved animals only when the two engaged in courteous dialogue. It is unlikely that Western societies will ever duplicate this particular, functionally conservationist vision of the universe. Nature, it seems to me, will be forever deaf and dumb in the presence of Judeo-Christian societies.

CHAPTER TWO

ONTARIO NATIVE PEOPLE AND THE EPIDEMICS OF 1634–1640

BRUCE G. TRIGGER

VALID SCIENTIFIC RESEARCH, including historical interpretation, requires a balance between theory and facts in which,
as Marvin Harris (1979) puts it, each side informs rather than
determines the other. Facts without theory signify nothing,
while theories, however attractive, which are untested by facts
remain mere speculations. The exceptionally detailed information that missionaries, government officials, and traders recorded concerning the Indian groups with whom the French
traded in the St. Lawrence Valley and the lower Great Lakes
region in the first half of the seventeenth century is especially
valuable for evaluating the controversial theories that Calvin
Martin has presented in *Keepers of the Game* (1978). These data
refer particularly to the Huron, a predominantly horticultural
Iroquoian people who lived in southern Ontario, and to a lesser
extent to their Iroquoian neighbors to the south and to the Algonkian-speaking Odawa (Ottawa), Nipissing, Algonkin, and
Montagnais peoples to the north and east. The latter groups
subsisted mainly by hunting and fishing. Although Martin (p.
185) believes that because the Iroquoians were primarily horticulturalists they were less concerned than were the Algonkian
hunters with the spiritual ramifications of wildlife extermination, he suggests that similar economic and spiritual motives
probably operated among both linguistic groupings (p. 8). The
Huron, like their Algonkian-speaking neighbors, treated the
bones of fish and animals that they caught with respect, to a
limited degree required menstruating women to avoid their
hunting and fishing equipment, and practiced a form of bear
ceremonialism. This suggests that information concerning the
Huron and neighboring Iroquoian groups is also relevant for
evaluating Martin's ideas.

Epidemics

The data we are considering were recorded only after a century of very poorly documented direct and indirect contact between Indians and Europeans. European goods seem to have been penetrating as far inland as southern Ontario in small quantities by the 1530s, and perhaps even earlier, and they increased in volume thereafter. Yet, to date, there is no hard evidence of major epidemics in the St. Lawrence Valley or southern Ontario during the sixteenth century. This and later more positive evidence warn us not to assume that every whaling or trading vessel that reached the St. Lawrence brought with it from Europe a cargo of lethal ailments. In 1535–36, about fifty inhabitants of the St. Lawrence Iroquoian village of Stadacona, near the site of Quebec City, died of some unspecified ailment while the French explorer, Jacques Cartier, and his crew wintered nearby. Some anthropologists have suggested that this and later unrecorded epidemics may have played a major role in the mysterious disappearance of the St. Lawrence Iroquoians (Fenton 1940:175). However, there is no historical or archaeological confirmation of this suggestion. While population trends in southern Ontario and New York State during the sixteenth century are an important subject for intensive archaeological research, there is presently no widespread evidence of a major decline in population at this time. Archaeologists have not noted unusually large ossuaries (or bone pits) in the proto-Huron sections of Ontario during the sixteenth century, while detailed studies of Seneca and Onondaga settlements have not recorded reductions in village size at that time (Tuck 1971). This does not exclude the possibility that changes of this sort occurred; however, it makes it intolerably speculative to base any interpretation of later Iroquoian behavior upon the assumption that they did.

Historical data from the seventeenth century are more abundant. They record only two minor epidemics in southern Ontario and the St. Lawrence Valley prior to 1634. In the summer of 1611, many Algonkin died of a fever (Biggar 1922–36, 2:207); in the winter of 1623–24 others died from disease and hunger (Wrong 1939:263). These may or may not have been outbreaks of European diseases. There is no evidence that the St. Lawrence Valley or southern Ontario was affected by the smallpox epidemic that ravaged the native peoples of New England between 1616 and 1619, or by earlier epidemics that may have struck the Maritime provinces.

In the summer of 1634 an epidemic, possibly of measles or some other European childhood illness, spread through the St. Lawrence Valley. By late autumn it had infected all of the Huron villages. At the same time, many Mohawk died from a disease that a Dutch visitor identified as smallpox (Jameson 1909:141). In the autumn of 1636, an outbreak of what seems to have been influenza spread from the St. Lawrence Valley to the Huron country. Prior to the next trading season the Huron and their neighbors were struck by a still more deadly malady which may have been the same one that earlier in 1637 had afflicted the Susquehannock (JR 14:9). This malady, which continued until the autumn of 1637, probably also killed many Wenroronon in New York State (JR 15:159). Finally, in the summer of 1639, much of eastern Canada was stricken by a highly lethal outbreak of smallpox (cf. Martin 1978:99), which the French claimed had been carried to the St. Lawrence Valley by Algonkins returning from a visit to the Abenaki (JR 16:101). A serious epidemic, perhaps a continuation of the smallpox, was reported to be raging among the Seneca when the Jesuit missionary Jean de Brébeuf visited the Neutral in the autumn of 1640 (JR 21:211). On the other hand, the Huron do not appear to have been afflicted by the contagious diseases that struck the Iroquois in 1646 and 1647 (JR 30:229, 273; 31:121).

This cycle of epidemics is the first one that at present can be demonstrated to have had a major impact on the demography of southern Ontario and the St. Lawrence Valley. By the time it was over, the Huron appear to have been reduced in number by about 50 percent, while hunter-gatherer populations to the north may have lost even more (Trigger 1976:499–602). It is therefore this cycle, and not a hypothetical earlier one, that must be used for assessing the impact that epidemics of European diseases had on native belief systems.

European Tools

By the time of these epidemics, even the Huron, who lived far inland, believed themselves to be dependent upon European goods to a considerable degree (JR 13:215–17). Groups such as the Montagnais and the Mohawk, who lived close to European trading posts, had become accustomed to using a still broader range of European goods and on a more lavish scale than did the Huron (Trigger 1976:358–60, 617–18). This dependence, which had grown up during a century of indirect and then direct contact with the French and which provided the basis for the fur trade, did not develop because, as Martin (p. 15) construes the traditional explanation, the Indians sought in the fashion of modern consumers to improve their "standard of living through material accumulation." Instead, it developed because native peoples clearly recognized that the possession of certain classes of European goods made life easier and more secure for them. Once they became familiar with the range of goods that the Europeans had to offer, they did not trade with them primarily to secure "baubles," as Martin (pp. 148–49) implies; instead, they sought to obtain items of considerable technological value. The Huron, for example, who had to transport goods for themselves and their many trading partners over a long and difficult route into the interior, sought first and foremost to obtain metal cutting tools, such as knives, awls, and axes, or the metal kettles from which, after they had worn out, such tools could be manufactured. They also sought to obtain or make metal arrowheads that could pierce the traditional wooden body armor worn by their enemies. Since the Iroquois were obtaining similar arrowheads from the Dutch, it was essential for the Huron to have these in order to maintain their military position. The Montagnais, as hunter-gatherers, also purchased dried peas, crackers, and sea biscuit, which substantially increased their chances of surviving the winter (Trigger 1976:409–13). In other words, the French trader Nicolas Denys (1908:441) was correct when he asserted that the Indians sought European goods "not so much for their novelty as for the convenience they derived therefrom."

The greater leisure resulting from the possession of metal cutting tools provided the economic basis for a cultural florescence among the tribes of eastern Canada in the seventeenth century. Among the Huron, this manifested itself in a more elaborate material culture and a more spectacular ritualism. The latter was evidenced most notably by the elaboration of the Feast of the Dead. By the 1630s, the Huron were dependent on the French, not in the sense that they did not still make pottery and stone tools, but because they had come to rely on European cutting tools for more efficient production, for military parity with their main enemies, and to maintain the trading alliances with neighboring tribes on which their security had now come to depend. Considering the practical advantages that the possession of a regular supply of European goods conferred on Indian groups, it is difficult to imagine why Martin (p. 184) should find it "odd" that native groups across North America were predisposed to promote and participate in the fur trade. Given the wide range of economic and military advantages resulting from the possession of European goods and the dangers attendant on not having them, it is hardly necessary to invoke obscure and poorly documented religious motivations to explain why the Indians participated in the fur trade. That these advantages and penalties should have become urgent enough to break down any controls against animal overkill that may have operated in the traditional religious system seems to me less astonishing than Martin's claim that as a response to unprecedented epidemics the Indians abandoned their traditional cosmology and much of their religious system.

Throughout the first half of the seventeenth century European goods generally remained scarce in relationship to the extensive and growing demand for them. Although native traders sought to obtain as many European goods as possible in return for each of their furs (Trigger 1976:362–64), they failed to establish exchange rates at which a conservationist hunting strategy would have permitted them to satisfy their demands. Under the trading monopoly which the French government generally enforced in the St. Lawrence Valley, these rates were generally even less favorable than in the Dutch and English colonies. By the beginning of the seventeenth century, the Montagnais at Tadoussac and the Algonkin in the Ottawa Valley were already acting as middlemen who traded European goods with tribes living farther inland. This allowed them to profit from a circular exchange of furs they did not have to trap for European goods they did not have to manufacture. Early in the seventeenth century, the Nipissing were recorded trading French goods as far north as James Bay, while the Odawa were carrying them westward to the shores of Lakes Michigan and Superior. After 1609, the Huron became the principal focus of all such trade that was centered in the Lake Huron region. None of these groups, whether the basis of their economy was horticulture or hunting and gathering, were dependent upon trapping to obtain the furs with which they purchased French goods. They were able to obtain far more furs as traders than they could have trapped within their own territories. As a result, they commanded far more wealth than did most of their neighbors. This provided the material basis for their cultural florescence.

Overkill

There is evidence that among some of these groups the depletion of beaver stocks was underway, or complete, prior to the epidemics of 1634–40. At the Sidey-Mackay site, which is a protohistoric Tionontati one probably dating towards the end of the sixteenth century, the high frequency of beaver bones and of stone and bone scrapers suggests that the trapping and processing of beaver skins were important activities (Wintemberg 1946:155). Huron sites in the Penetanguishene Peninsula likewise indicate an increase in beaver hunting around 1570 to 1620 and a decline thereafter (Trigger 1976:350). Gabriel Sagard (1866:585) and Paul Le Jeune (JR 8:57) confirm that by about 1630 beaver had been hunted to extinction within the Hurons' hunting territories. This did not appear to trouble the Huron, since by that time their trading networks were sufficiently elaborated that they could obtain from other tribes all the beaver skins that they needed to purchase goods from the French.

While it is uncertain whether or not beaver had been eliminated within the hunting territories of the Five Nations Iroquois by 1640, the furs that could be taken from these territories clearly no longer sufficed to purchase all of the European goods that the Iroquois wished to obtain. The Iroquois sought to obtain more furs by robbing them from other tribes and by expanding their hunting territories at the expense of other peoples. These raids gradually extended over a larger area and involved the seizure of larger quantities of furs. It is also clear that beaver stocks had been exhausted in the Iroquois heartland south of Lake Ontario sometime before 1671 (O'Callaghan and Fernow 1856–87, 9:80).

In the late 1630s, fear that the beaver population of the St. Lawrence Valley would be wiped out led Father Le Jeune to advocate that specific hunting territories be assigned to each Montagnais family in order to encourage conservation. The situation had become especially acute among the Montagnais who lived near the growing French settlement at Quebec. Unlike the Montagnais at Tadoussac or the Algonkin bands farther west, these peoples did not live in an area from which as middlemen they were able to barter European goods among Indians living in the interior. Hence, in their desire to emulate the lifestyle of their neighbors, they overhunted their own land and then, as the beaver disappeared, became a sullen and unwelcome burden to the French trading company. To cope with this situation, the Society of Jesus founded a mission at Sillery in 1638, where these Montagnais were encouraged to settle and live a Christian life. To enable them to do this, the society provided them with houses, food, and clothing purchased with funds the Jesuits had collected for such mission work (JR 8:57–59).

It would appear that the Huron and the Iroquois both exterminated the beaver in their respective hunting territories after they no longer had to rely on these territories to supply them with beaver skins. By contrast, the Montagnais at Quebec seem to have exterminated them in a desperate short-term effort to emulate the living standard of their more affluent neighbors in the St. Lawrence Valley. Among the Huron, the extermination of beaver was complete prior to the epidemics of 1634–40, and it was clearly well underway among the Montagnais prior to this time. Whatever breakdown occurred in traditional belief systems that may have limited the trapping of beaver seems to have been a response to economic developments rather than a result of cognitive changes associated with major outbreaks of European diseases.

Sickness and Religion

There is strong evidence that shamanistic curing practices were an important aspect of northern Iroquoian religion in prehistoric times (Tooker 1960), and probably among neighboring Algonkian-speaking peoples as well. It is therefore highly improbable that shamanism and healing societies developed among the Huron mainly as a response to epidemic diseases introduced by Europeans (cf. Brasser 1971:263). There is no direct evidence that the Huron associated disease with animal spirits. Among other causes, they believed that their female creator Aataentsic, who also made men die and thereafter had charge of their souls, caused epidemics.

It seems to me that the association between animals and disease among many American Indian groups, and especially groups that depended on hunting for subsistence, can be explained in more general and convincing terms than their cognizance of zoonotic infection, although I do not mean to imply that they were necessarily unaware of such connections. The French observed that famine and disease tended to occur together, especially among hunting peoples (JR 11:197; Wrong 1939:263). Failure to secure adequate game during the winter undermined the vitality of Indian groups and exposed them to the ravages of disease. Alternatively, epidemics, whether of European or indigenous origin, interfered with hunting and could easily lead to starvation. These experiences, often repeated, seem to provide a more general basis for associating hunting, animals, and disease than does the phenomenon of zoonotic infection.

Martin (p. 52) postulates that during major outbreaks of European diseases the Indians had recourse to their usual techniques of curing, including shamanism. One by one, they exhausted their traditional repertoire of cures, and when these failed to save them, their faith in shamanism and their view of the universe and of their relationship to it were shattered. This view ascribes a rigidity, inflexibility, and narrow-mindedness to native religion that does not appear to correspond with the facts. The *Jesuit Relations* clearly indicate that during the major epidemics, curing rituals among the Huron were dynamic and innovative. The spread of illness encouraged a general upsurge in healing practices. Curing societies performed their rituals in every village, and shamans sought to enhance their reputations by divining the cause of the illness and prescribing effective cures. For example, in 1636, a shaman named Tsondacouané, who was in much repute around the Huron town of Onnentisati, entered into communion with various spirits of the surrounding landscape and on their recommendation prescribed the performance of rituals by the Awataerohi curing society and the erection of straw masks over the doors of houses and human figures on the roofs (JR 13:227–33). Later, he advised that the dead should be buried in the ground for a time before being placed in bark tombs in the village cemeteries (JR 13:259). Another cure was revealed to the shaman Tehorenhaegnon after a twelve-day fast on the shores of Nottawasaga Bay. In January 1637, he shared his power with three other shamans, who were deputized to practice his cure. At the climax of this ritual, the sick were sprinkled with water from a kettle, while the shamans followed fanning them with a turkey wing that Tehorenhaegnon had supplied (JR 13:237–43).

Many Huron at first regarded the Jesuits as members of a French curing society. Some of them requested baptism as a cure for their illnesses, on the same basis as they sought the assistance of other shamans or curing societies. Later they shunned it, when they observed that most Hurons who had been baptized died. What they had not understood was that the Jesuits normally baptized without prolonged instruction only adults who were in imminent danger of dying. The Huron shamans also incorporated elements of Christian practice into their curing rituals, as Tehorenhaegnon may have been doing in the example cited above. Yet in doing so they interpreted these elements in a thoroughly Huron fashion. The Huron frequently adopted rituals or elements of rituals from other Indian groups (Trigger 1976:76); hence borrowing these ones is no evidence that they yet regarded the Jesuits as being different from other shamans.

The Huron appear to have been quite pragmatic in their evaluation of both rituals and shamans. Old ones that did not produce cures were abandoned, and the effectiveness of new ones was carefully monitored by both the shamans and their clients (JR 13:243). Yet the rejection of individual rituals as being unsuccessful did not, as Martin (p. 52) assumes, lead to a loss of faith in the traditional religion or the premises on which it was based. Indeed, it spurred the Huron to search within the context of available religious knowledge for specific rituals that did work. This process continued throughout each epidemic, and it seems likely that some rituals meant to halt the epidemic actually acquired a reputation for effectiveness as the mortality rate eventually declined.

The Huron religion appears to have emerged intact at the end of the epidemics, except for the loss of some esoteric ritual knowledge that was privately owned and failed to be transmitted as a result of the unprecedented rate of mortality (JR 8:145–47). The increasing number of conversions that were effected by the Jesuits among the Huron after 1640 was largely accomplished by their manipulation of material rewards rather than the result of Huron disillusionment with their traditional religion. Only Christians were allowed to buy guns, Christians trading with the French were treated with more respect than non-Christians, and trade goods were sold to Christians at lower prices than to other Indians. Large-scale nominal conversions occurred later in the decade, as the Huron were compelled to seek Jesuit protection from increasing Iroquois attacks. The Algonkin and Montagnais likewise submitted to baptism only when they found themselves in dire poverty or when Iroquois raids forced them to seek shelter near French strongholds.

Apostasy was common when the political situation improved (Trigger 1976:699–724).

Thus it appears that the native religions of eastern Canada had sufficient resilience to survive the epidemics more or less intact. A parallel might be drawn with the Black Death in fourteenth-century Europe. It gave rise to many aberrant short-term religious movements but did not, by itself, in the long run significantly alter the role played by Christianity in European civilization. What undermined the traditional religions of eastern Canada were the growing dependence of native peoples on French goods and military protection and the exploitation of this dependence by the Jesuit missionaries to compel the Indians to practice Christianity.

Witchcraft

The evidence concerning the epidemics of 1634–40 also refutes Martin's suggestion (p. 146) that the Indians could not have conceived of such widespread epidemics as being caused by witchcraft. Nor is it true that the French were not accused of practicing such witchcraft until after the Indians had been ravaged by European diseases for some time (p. 154). The Micmac probably conceptualized in terms of witchcraft their accusations, recorded by Father Pierre Biard soon after 1611, that French traders had attempted to poison them and had sold them adulterated food (JR 3:105–7). When the Indians failed to arrest the epidemics with their regular pharmacopia and traditional rituals that sought to appease various spirits, they began to fear that they were victims of powerful witchcraft. Hence they searched for the source of this witchcraft and for ways to counteract it. At first, the Huron accused individual members of their own society, thereby hoping to persuade them to desist. As the epidemics grew worse, a number of these suspected witches were slain. Most of these executions were carried out by young warriors at the command of their war chiefs, witches being regarded as equivalent to foreign enemies (Trigger 1976:537).

As the epidemics grew still more serious, the Indians began to accuse other tribes of practicing witchcraft, apparently assuming that sorcery on an intertribal level was more potent than that practiced by individuals. The Nipissing, for example, blamed the epidemics on the Kichesipirini, or Islander, Algonkin. They feared that the Islander Algonkin had afflicted all surrounding nations with pestilence because these neighboring groups had recently refused to help the Algonkin avenge wrongs that they had suffered at the hands of the Iroquois (JR 13:211).

Eventually, however, the widespread distribution of the epidemics and the observation that many of them had begun at the French trading posts and followed French trade goods into the interior (JR 11:197) led the Indians to conclude that the French were the cause of these illnesses. Since the French apparently had the power to remain well or to cure themselves of these diseases, it seemed inexplicable, unless they were deliberately seeking to kill the Indians, that they did not use their powers to cure them as well. A remorseless logic, innocent of the varying susceptibility of different populations to the same diseases, concluded that the French were sorcerers with unprecedented power who were using their witchcraft to destroy the Indians. Their attempts to determine why the French wished to do this dramatized the major and minor stresses that beset French-Indian relations at this time. The impoverished and dependent Montagnais who lived near Quebec were convinced that the French were exterminating them in order to take possession of their land (JR 16:93). The Huron had never understood why the French insisted that they allow the Jesuits, whom they now regarded as especially powerful sorcerers and whom they disliked because they so often spoke about souls and death, to live in their midst. They now decided that the French had sent the Jesuits to exterminate the Indians.

It was feared that this might have been done to retaliate for the murder of the French trader, Etienne Brûlé by the Huron in 1633. Various statements that the Jesuits made were interpreted as confirming such suspicions, while further confirmation came to the Huron in their dreams, which were regarded as being of great divinatory importance. Baptism and the food and drugs that the Jesuits distributed to the Indians were believed to be among the ways that the Jesuits bewitched their victims. Their pictures of hell were interpreted as representations of the fevers and torments with which they afflicted the Indians.

The Nipissing offered the Jesuits a belt containing 2,400 wampum beads as compensation for a belt that they had stolen from Brûlé, if the Jesuits would spare them from the epidemic (JR 14:101–3). Likewise, the Tionontati offered the Jesuits a beaver robe if the Jesuits would stop illness emanating from their chapel. The Huron were divided as to whether it was preferable to try to placate the Jesuits or to destroy them. By accusing them of witchcraft, they hoped to frighten them into abandoning their witchcraft. However, the fur trade was so important to the Huron that French threats to terminate it if any priests were slain sufficed to protect the Jesuits and their workmen from more than an occasional nonlethal assault, a response which also indicates the great extent to which the Huron now believed themselves to be dependent on the French. It seems significant that alongside this detailed evidence that native peoples attributed the epidemics of 1634–40 to witchcraft, there is no reference whatever to a breakdown of good relations between the Huron or their Algonkian-speaking neighbors and any animal spirits.

Volume of Trade

There is, however, one piece of indirect evidence that might be construed as support for Martin's theory. As mentioned before, our data suggest that between 1634 and 1640 the Huron population was cut by about 50 percent, while the northern hunters, who supplied them with furs, may have experienced an even higher level of mortality. Yet the number of furs that were being supplied to the French in the 1640s seems to have been even greater than it had been prior to 1634 (Trigger 1976:603). This might suggest that, following the epidemics, the northern hunters unleashed a "war against the animals" which led to more beaver being killed by each hunter, even though there was no greater per capita need for European trade goods than before. Yet this is not the only possible explanation, and there is no particular evidence to support it. The deaths of many hunters may have made it possible for those who survived to trap more beaver than before with less than a proportional increase in effort. Since most of the hunting groups that lived in the interior had probably been poorly provided with European goods prior to the epidemics, their wish to obtain more may have motivated these survivors to trap beaver more extensively. Their dependence on European goods also may have been increased by a widespread loss of technological skills which reportedly occurred because many old people, who were masters of them, were dying from European diseases (JR 8:145–47). Alternatively, the Huron and other native groups occupying a middleman position in the fur trade may have compensated for the deaths of hunter-gatherers by extending their trading networks over a greater geographical area. As many Hurons were engaged in trading with the French after the epidemics as had been before, and perhaps more (Trigger 1976:605). It is therefore likely that the Huron were committing a larger percentage of their manpower to the fur trade at this time than they had done previously. To a considerable degree this behavior may reflect increasing Huron dependence on the French as a result of the growing pressure of the Iroquois. Annual quotas may now have been set as much by French expectations as by increasing Huron needs.

Conclusions

We have not been able to discover in the French literature concerning the St. Lawrence Valley and southern Ontario in the first half of the seventeenth century any direct evidence to support Martin's assumption that failure to cope with epidemic diseases led to a spiritual crisis followed by a war against the animals. Our data support the materialist interpretation that the Indians valued European goods because those goods made life easier for them. It appears that, regardless of what their religious beliefs had been, in many instances they were prepared to hunt beaver to extinction as the only or even the most expedient way to obtain these goods. The epidemics were explained in terms of witchcraft, for which the French were often held responsible. Yet the growing dependence of the Indians on their European trading partners for tools and weapons which in many cases had become vital to their survival did not permit them to break off relations with these partners.

I do not deny the importance of trying to understand the fur trade in terms of how it was perceived by the Indians. Nor do I deny that in some instances idealist explanations of historical phenomena may be valid. It appears, however, that materialist explanations, which view human behavior primarily as a response to the problems of mortal existence, account for such activities more often than do idealist ones. Hence, on general grounds, I am not surprised that the particular data reviewed here do not sustain Martin's thesis.

References Cited

Biggar, H. P., ed.
1922–36   The Works of Samuel de Champlain. 6 vols.
            Toronto: The Champlain Society.

Brasser, T. J. C.
1971   Group Identification along a Moving Frontier. Ver-
            handlungen des XXXVIII Internationalen
            Amerikanistenkongresses, Munich. Vol. 2,
            pp. 261–65.

Denys, Nicolas
1908   The Description and Natural History of the
            Coasts of North America. W. F. Ganong, ed.
            Toronto: The Champlain Society.

Fenton, W. N.
1940   Problems Arising from the Historic Northeastern
            Position of the Iroquois. Smithsonian Mis-
            cellaneous Collections 100:159–252.

Harris, Marvin
1979   Cultural Materialism. New York: Random House.

Jameson, J. F., ed.
1909   Narratives of New Netherlands, 1609–1664. New
            York: Scribner's.

JR. See Thwaites.

Martin, Calvin
1978   Keepers of the Game: Indian-Animal Relation-
            ships and the Fur Trade. Berkeley: University of
            California Press.

O'Callaghan, E. B., and B. Fernow, eds.
1856–87   Documents Relative to the Colonial History of the
            State of New York. 15 vols. Albany: Weed,
            Parsons.

Sagard, Gabriel
1866   Histoire du Canada. Paris: Edwin Tross.
Thwaites, R. G., ed.
1896–1901 The Jesuit Relations and Allied Documents. 73
           vols. Cleveland: Burrows.
Tooker, Elisabeth
1960   Three Aspects of Northern Iroquoian Culture
           Change. Pennsylvania Archaeologist 30(2):65–71.
Trigger, B. G.
1976   The Children of Aataentsic: A History of the
           Huron People to 1660. 2 vols. Montreal: McGill-
           Queen's University Press.
Tuck, J. A.
1971   Onondaga Iroquois Prehistory: A Study in Settle-
           ment Archaeology. Syracuse: Syracuse University
           Press.
Wintemberg, W. J.
1946   The Sidey-Mackay Village Site. American Antiq-
           uity 11:154–82.
Wrong, G. M., ed.
1939   The Long Journey to the Country of the Hurons.
           Toronto: The Champlain Society.

CHAPTER THREE

NORTHEASTERN INDIAN CONCEPTS OF CONSERVATION AND THE FUR TRADE: A CRITIQUE OF CALVIN MARTIN'S THESIS

CHARLES A. BISHOP

CALVIN MARTIN has presented a provocative thesis linking postcontact animal overexploitation with changes in the northeastern Indian ideological system. Although his argument is not supported by the historical data and contains a number of unfounded assumptions often based upon a questionable methodology, *Keepers of the Game* remains an important book because Martin has addressed himself to issues of major theoretical significance. Furthermore, he is one of the few historians who has attempted to deal with the issue of the role of ideology in Indian culture change. Through his focus upon Indian cognition and how this was related to behavior both in prehistoric times and during the fur trade era, he has made a number of us rethink our own positions. The purpose here will be to attempt to correct and refine his interpretations in the light of the ethnohistorical information on the Northern Algonkian region and current ethnological theory.

Disease, Ideology, and Indian
Exploitative Patterns

Much of what Martin says about aboriginal Algonkian religion appears to be correct, and he presents an interesting and fresh perspective on a poorly understood period of Amerindian history. Further, few would argue with his basic point of departure, that European diseases, the fur trade, and missionary activities profoundly altered ecological, territorial, and social relationships. What has excited heated commentary is his controversial hypothesis that Indians adopted an apostatizing mood in reaction to the effects of these diseases, which Martin assumes they blamed on animals and subsequently overexploited game. While it is quite likely that European diseases did spread in advance of direct contact with whites in some regions, such as along the Atlantic seaboard, it is highly doubtful that this occurred everywhere. There is no evidence to suggest that the first serious epidemics were experienced before many groups of Indians were intimately involved in the fur trade. The absence of direct evidence, of course, is no proof that epidemics did not occur. It does, however, weaken Martin's argument for Indian antipathy towards game among all groups.

Similarly, Martin makes the valid but overextended claim that Indians would have recognized that some animal diseases can be transmitted to humans, and thus, would have blamed game keepers. It is possible that the effects of disease in some instances could have caused doubts about the intentions of game spirits. Because of the selectivity of Martin's data, however, I remain unconvinced that Indians originally engaged in the fur trade simply "to vanquish [their] enemies, the treacherous wildlife" (p. 148). In fact, there are some logical and empirical reasons against such a view. On logical grounds alone one could argue with equal force, and in the absence of concrete data, that Indians stricken by epidemics might have been especially courteous to game spirits, since warring against them could have been construed as creating additional illness. Martin is also aware of the empirical evidence that Algonkians in the St. Lawrence Valley accused the French of spreading diseases and that whole villages were deserted in fear of these. But he explains these examples away by arguing that they occurred *after* Indians had already been ravaged by prior epidemics which had been blamed on game keepers (p. 54n). He falls back on the nonfalsifiable logic that since there were no white witnesses to these events, they cannot be disproven. However, neither can they be proven. Furthermore, he presents data that the Indian relationship to resources did not depend upon religious sanctions alone, but on deliberate manipulation of the habitat through burning, clearing, and so on. Finally, Martin's argument, like his use of the data, seems overly nice at times, particularly when he argues for a rejection of the ideological system to explain the slaughter of game and then testifies that the slaughter was, in fact, ideologically generated. An inversion such as he would have us accept is not easy; I can think of no comparable example, say, in Christianity or Islam.

Actually, there is a serious methodological flaw in this argument. If northeastern Algonkians had been so thoroughly despiritualized even before European acculturative changes occurred, how is it that early and later recorders of Indian beliefs (interpreted by Martin to be aboriginal) were able to collect so much data on these? That such data were still abundantly available and presumably represented a relatively unaltered belief system is accepted by Martin himself, since he draws on these extensively to interpret the aboriginal system. It would be logically inconsistent to use such materials and then argue that the beliefs were already bastardized. Yet one must ask; If Indians were despiritualized before direct contact, how has Martin methodologically sorted out that which was aboriginal from that which was not? He is not unaware of this problem, and contends that "complete repudiation [of traditional beliefs] must have been rare" (p. 154), and that "fragments of the aboriginal hunting and, broader yet, spiritual complex survive today" (p. 151).

Because he accepts that elements of the prehistoric belief system survived, he does not hesitate to draw upon the field data of such twentieth-century scholars as A. I. Hallowell, Frank Speck, Adrian Tanner, and Harvey Feit. But there is another reason why he maintains that it is legitimate to use more recent evidence. With the emergence of the Algonkian family hunting territory system, dormant aboriginal spiritual sentiments resurfaced under conditions where game conservation had again become practical. Thus, even though the relationship between Man and Nature had been corrupted, the new form of land tenure became a source for a revitalized prehistoric conservation ethic. In order for this to have happened, however, these "aboriginal" sentiments must have replaced the "mongrel outlook," that mixture of "native traditions and beliefs with a European rationale and motivation" where the Indian was no longer "the sensitive fellow-member of a symbolic world" (p. 61). In sum, Martin is arguing that two major religious transformations occurred after contact. Initially, in reaction to diseases blamed on animals, Indians apostatized, which means literally that they abandoned their religion or at least developed a "mongrel" one. Later, they reverted to more pristine beliefs and practices concerning nature in response to the development of a new land tenure system. I find this argument preposterous.

First, I would argue that the man-animal relationship in the prehistoric period differed radically from that in more recent historical times. Precontact Indians would not have overexploited their habitat because there was no reason to do so: resources were apparently relatively abundant and easy to obtain. In contrast, the institutionalization of the family hunting territory system was an adaptive strategy often encouraged by the fur traders (Bishop 1974:210) to prevent overexploitation given limited and greatly reduced resources, especially of fur-bearers, which had become necessary to survival under exchange-dependency conditions. Although the Indian rationale for not killing game was often phrased in ideological terms, the conditions making this rationale strategically sound were quite different from those characterizing the aboriginal state, insofar as it is possible to reconstruct that state from the early records.

Second, while it may be true that the Indian belief system suffered some severe shocks as a result of white intervention, one of them being due to disease, it does not follow that Indians turned against game or became despiritualized. The synthesis of Indian beliefs and white economic rationale, the unfortunately labeled "mongrel outlook," does not mean that Indians were "despiritualized"; synthesization need not be denigrated as mongrelization, and adaptive change is not necessarily apostatization. True, there are some good indications that Indian religion among some groups underwent modification during the early historic period. In the upper Great Lakes area seventeenth-century Algonkian Feasts of the Dead grew increasingly elaborate after contact; and the later emergence of the Midewiwin among the Ojibwa seems to have been a response to sociopolitical developments southwest of Lake Superior (Hickerson 1960, 1963). Both, however, emphasized traditional values in new contexts or forms and under new socioeconomic conditions. Despite such changes, it is generally accepted that various twentieth-century ethnologists have been able to document a fair segment of what appears to be an aboriginal belief system, albeit with certain important modifications. But the modern presence of aboriginal elements cannot be explained simply as the reappearance or revival of a long dormant pre-Columbian conservationist ethic. Such an argument is surely less elegant than one that accepts the existing evidence for a belief system which, throughout much of the eastern Algonkian area, appears to have been continuously maintained until quite recently, except where Christian proselitizing efforts were strong.

In sum, while diseases devastated and decimated some groups, profoundly modifying social organizational features and ecological relationships, the effects were very unevenly felt both in space and time. Thus, while *in some cases* animals may have been blamed, the argument is unsupportable as a general explanation of hunting and trapping practices under fur trade conditions. There is no hard evidence that (1) all or even most Indians apostatized, or (2) that a pre-Columbian game ethic lay dormant for what amounted to nearly two centuries until a new land tenure system emerged.

The Fur Trade and Indian Motives

At the heart of Martin's argument for Indian involvement in the fur trade and their heavy exploitation of game is a search for Indian motives to explain postcontact events documented in the historical literature. Martin asks what the fur trade meant "to the Indian partner in this transaction, within his cultural context" and how we are to "interpret the dynamics of the fur trade within [the Indian's] cosmic frame of reference" (p. 2). The questions are well phrased and, indeed, crucial ones both from the perspective of our understanding of Indian involvement in that trade and in terms of even broader theoretical issues. That is why *Keepers of the Game* is such a notable book. That Martin's answers are often inadequate makes the task of resolving the issues no less important.

Martin begins by rejecting the "economic man" view to explain why Indians hunted game to near-extinction. This view, which accounts for Indian participation in the fur trade in terms of what others have interpreted to mean the perceived superiority of European trade goods, is too simplistic, says Martin, because it ignores the native belief and value system. With this, there can be little debate. However, to argue that animals were killed in revenge for the diseases they spread and because Indians had apostatized is equally simplistic.

The problem is that Martin erroneously assumes that a respect for game keepers would, in the absence of some factor eradicating that respect, inhibit Indians from killing game to acquire European material goods. What he fails to recognize is that Indians can have practical and pragmatic wants which are not necessarily in conflict with beliefs about the animal world and how it is to be exploited. Thus, motives to acquire new material items need not cancel out or replace attitudes of respect towards game. Martin's view that such an ideological transformation occurred seems based, in part, upon the post hoc evidence that an intensification of productive efforts ultimately led to diminishing returns. However, to assume that an increase in production would lead automatically to this, or that Indians were aware of its ultimate consequences, is unfounded. It implies that an ideological superstructure originated as a justification designed to inhibit overexploitation, when no such conceptual apparatus appears to have existed. While Martin's confusion on this point would seem to stem from his rejection of formal economic theory in favor of substantivism, he may, of course, be correct in denying capitalistic drives or "bourgeois impulses" to native Algonkians. It is difficult to determine exactly what values were held by seventeenth-century Algonkians, or what new attitudes were engendered by trade items. We can speculate, however.

Initially, trade goods were probably perceived as luxury items which could be obtained relatively easily by groups near trading centers. No doubt Indians recognized the technological superiority of many items which "enhanced convenience" (p. 154). However, to state as does Martin that these trade goods were perceived as being of less value to Indians than to whites is debatable. Certainly their technological importance was less during the early years, since, except in a few limited areas, Indians had not grown dependent on them for survival. Nevertheless, the social and political purposes to which these goods were put were very important indeed. Not only did Indians appreciate the special qualities of trade materials, whether they be technological or not (as in the case of alcohol and tobacco), but they were able to employ these goods to elaborate on aboriginal values. That is, by acquiring these luxury items, Indian leaders could acquire greater prestige and authority among their kinsmen through redistribution, an elaboration of the value of generosity for political gain. The descriptions of seventeenth-century Algonkian Feasts of the Dead make this abundantly clear. These ceremonials so closely parallel nineteenth-century Northwest Coast potlatches as to suggest that similar motives were involved in both cases.

Adam Smith in 1776 (1950, 1:17) argued that when a producer disposes of his products in order to exchange them for goods of an equivalent value produced by others, he is involved in a market economy. This surely was the case in the trade between Indians and whites, although even here some qualifications are required. The question is, then, What was the nature of the flow of goods at the next stage in the system, when these European commodities were circulated within and between Indian groups? Were these goods invested as a form of social security for some future time when individuals could call upon reciprocity? Or was the accumulation of prestige and power the aim? Or both? If either, then it may be asked why Indians did not exert themselves to trap or travel to the trading post more than they seemingly did. There are numerous instances in the historical records where Indians refused to trap despite constant urging by traders. Martin himself supplies the answer when he approvingly cites Sahlins's argument that Indians also put a high value on leisure. It is clear that not all Indians were able to acquire prestige, nor would they continue to labor for pelts once their immediate wants were satisfied. Some, however, who controlled leadership positions were willing to put in more effort than others in order to maintain their positions. Among the nineteenth-century Carrier of Stuart Lake, Chief Kwah was reported to have had to do much of the work on the salmon weir himself (Bishop 1980). His fellow villagers would often do no more than the bare minimum. But Kwah was a "man of note" for whom extra labor was a necessary prerequisite for the prestige he gained. Also, the others might have perceived that their efforts would not have brought them personal gain, but would only have added to Kwah's status, thus making them more his followers. So what did they have to gain except greater control by Kwah?

But the value placed upon leisure was not the only reason that productive efforts did not increase exponentially. Cree middlemen in the eighteenth-century fur trade would not have brought more pelts to the trading post had the value of furs been increased (Ray 1974; Ray and Freeman 1978). They would, in fact, have brought fewer furs to satisfy the same wants. As Ray has shown, there were several reasons for this. First, Cree canoes could carry only a limited quantity of furs and trade goods; so until traders occupied the hinterland west of Hudson Bay during the late eighteenth century, quantities brought to Bayside posts did not increase significantly. Also, as indicated, extra work would have been required, work which Indians were not willing to do. As it was, these lengthy treks were exhausting, and Indians frequently complained of food shortages en route. Third, a less obvious reason may have been that Indian middlemen did not wish to flood the hinterland with trade goods, thereby creating a devaluation. That is, they could keep the value high by limiting the quantity of materials being distributed. There are good data indicating that the middleman markup on trade goods was extremely high, at times as much as 1000 percent! Since these Indian traders knew well the value of the goods which they received, they certainly must have been aware of the profit which they were making. But again we must question whether the profit was gauged in terms of the amount of wealth to be hoarded. This seems not to have been the case. Nevertheless, both economic and political reasons were involved. On the one hand, the more followers a trade chief could muster, the more prestige and political clout he acquired, both at the trading post and among his followers. On the other, these trade goods were in many instances technologically superior, a fact recognized by Indians. Thus, Indian middlemen had to balance the quantity of furs to be gathered with the goods and profits to be gained and the labor to be expended so as to maximize prestige, trade materials, and efficiency under the conditions which prevailed at any given time.

When viewed within this context, then, formal economic theory is applicable. And it is applicable in terms of the Indians' value system—to remain secure, to be generous to one's followers, to avoid unnecessary labor, and at the same time to enhance prestige and to acquire desired and useful goods. I would argue further that Indians involved in the early fur trade wished to alter their behavior only to the extent that they could maximize traditional values through the medium of new goods. The effects of the fur trade from the Indian perspective, then, is a good example of Romer's Rule applied to a cultural context. That is, "the initial survival value of a favorable innovation is conservative, in that it renders possible the maintenance of a traditional way of life in the face of changed circumstances" (Hockett and Ascher 1964:137). Thus, Indians evolved new adaptive strategies within a new ecological-exchange setting so as to attempt to maintain continuity with the past. Unfortunately, in the long run, they were unsuccessful for reasons well documented in the ethnohistorical record (Leacock 1954; Hickerson 1962; Bishop 1974).

In sum, Indians coveted trade goods both for their technological qualities and also to gain prestige and power through redistribution, or power through enhanced states of intoxication (Dailey 1968). The desire to acquire trade goods was strong although the purposes to which these were put often differed significantly from those of Europeans. Antipathy toward game played an insignificant role at best throughout the entire postcontact period.

A basic unanswered question is why Indians wanted prestige in the first place. Even in later years when the family hunting territory system was in effect, and when conservation practices had become mandatory, Indians who brought in the greatest number of valuable furs were considered important men among their fellows. Despite changes in adapative strategies, and under conditions where trade goods had become necessary to survival, prestige was a virtue. Thus, unless we revert to some sociobiological argument that all humans innately value prestige, this issue must remain unresolved. Perhaps Lionel Tiger will resolve it for us!

Before turning to the issues of overexploitation and the conservation ethic, one final point needs clarification. This concerns the impact of European technology on the Indian way of life. Certainly, Martin is correct in stating that "it would be unreasonable to suggest that iron revolutionized Indian hunting" (p. 16) insofar as this applied to the early years of the fur trade. However, the adoption of European materials, especially metal ones, had a cumulative effect. Not only did these come to replace prehistoric ones, but in doing so, memory of how to produce the latter was irretrievably lost. But perhaps more important, the quest for these items led to alterations in man-land relationships often resulting in geographical circumscription and, as Martin notes, a marked decline in the population of certain animal species. As a result of these changes, Indians became dependent upon trapping as a means of obtaining trade goods both for trapping itself and for other necessities (such as blankets and cloth in the absence of animal hides), as was the case among the mid-nineteenth-century Northern Ojibwa (Bishop 1974). Under these conditions trade materials made the difference between acquiring furs and food and thereby satisfying basic needs, or suffering severe deprivation and even death. The trends leading to this situation had begun much earlier. Martin (p. 106) notes David Thompson's early-nineteenth-century remark that Indian tools were incapable of breaking through beaver lodges. While it is apparent that Martin is aware of these data, it seems to me that he might have been somewhat more precise in spelling out the processes leading to dependency upon European materials. In sum, the cultural and ecological context, particularly as it altered temporally and regionally, in which European tools functioned should have been more carefully specified. In fact, this is a constant problem throughout the book since Martin tends to compress nearly 400 years of cultural history into a homogenized "ethnographic present." It is somewhat quixotic for an historian to have abandoned the careful methods of historiography in favor of a methodology employed by early- to mid-twentieth-century anthropologists, one which has come under severe criticism (Hickerson 1967, 1970).

Overkill, Conservation, the Fur Trade and Territoriality

I agree with Martin that it was possible for prehistoric Indians to overexploit game resources, given their traditional technological knowledge. The fact that they were able to do this in the postcontact period, albeit with the aid of certain European implements, tends to support this; for one cannot attribute this overexploitation solely to the new technology, as Martin correctly argues. Nevertheless, prehistoric Algonkians did not overexploit their habitat, since hunting was generally reported in the early records to have been a reliable activity (pp. 125–27) (except near certain trading posts where hunting strategies had been altered by the contact situation). But was this because aboriginal Indians were aware that overhunting would have endangered a species, or because they recognized that they would produce less game for the same or greater effort? It is here where Martin's argument tends to confuse the two. On one hand, he tells us that it is erroneous to assign the American Indian a Western-sounding conservation ethic, but on the other, he argues that the "fur-trading Indian . . . was simply too skilled a hunter to overlook the ultimate consequences of wildlife overkill" (p. 3). The former can be interpreted to mean that since a Western conservation ethic was absent, so also was a concept of overkill, which is probably correct; while the latter tends to imply that Indians were conscious that game could be overexploited, which is extremely doubtful. It is more likely that they were attempting to maximize hunting potential. This could be obtained both by restricting human population growth and by remaining mobile. In regard to the latter, the records indicate that early contact Indians moved to new hunting regions long before game had been exterminated from an area being exploited. The belief system, I would add, was geared to reinforcing maximum efficiency in subsistence activities so as to avoid "the wages of poverty" (Sahlins 1972:33–34). So was Northern Algonkian social structure. The apparent emphasis on matrilocality (Bishop and Krech 1980), which dispersed male hunters, maximized political cohesion so as to permit bands the option of utilizing a number of alternative regions available through dispersed agnatic links. Hence, "social structure [was] an emanation of the systemic attempt to limit . . . penalties within the capacity of the processes of production" (Harris 1979:241).

Both the aboriginal and the early historical Indian probably lacked a well-defined concept of overexploitation. For the Indian to have had such a concept, a macro concept of biomass systemics would have had to have been present. But it is usually assumed that because of their apparent affluence tribal peoples did not have a concept of limited good (or limited goods) until long after they had become enmeshed in a European mercantile trade system, at which time resources had become depleted. Martin himself supplies data supporting this when he notes the belief that animals could be continuously regenerated through proper treatment of their remains (p. 36), but he rejects the idea that this could have led to overkill on the grounds that excessive hunting would have offended game spirits. But, it may be asked, why would prehistoric Indians have wanted to engage in excessive hunting when leisure was so highly valued? There was little or no reason why Indians should have "feared" game spirit reprisal when they would not have killed unnecessarily. It was not that Indians were opposed to killing large numbers of animals so long as game keepers were properly propitiated and so long as exploitation was viewed positively—that is, so long as material benefits outweighed material costs. Therefore, caution must be exhibited when one employs such loaded Western terms as "overkill" and "overexploitation." In restrospect, it is easy to see the results of this overkill, but it is unlikely that the perceptual environment of the Indians who were engaged in the early fur trade included such a concept. In later times, however, Indians may have embraced this concept. Thus, contrary to Martin, I would argue that the twentieth-century field-derived information that Indians were obligated to limit their kills in order to prevent a decline in animal populations was indeed of recent origin, "a case of white-induced conservationism" (p. 83n) and a diagnostic feature of the family hunting territory system.It may be true, though, that the integration of traditional beliefs with a new form of land tenure functioned to preserve both the belief system in a modified form as well as the animal population. But preservation is not the same as revitalization, since Indian beliefs seemingly did not languish during the period of heavy exploitation. The Indian belief system seems simply to have incorporated a concept of overkill. Thus, an inability to acquire game could be explained as being the result of a breach of a taboo involving animals as in former times, or a scarcity of animals due to overhunting, or certain natural factors such as snow conditions, temperature, and so on. The reason given by Indians would depend upon the particular circumstances. Among the possibilities was the new awareness that previous hunting practices could deplete game and affect future success or failure.

Furthermore, if Indians lacked a concept of overkill, one which must be based upon the notion that resources are finite, then it is also conceivable that some Pleistocene extinctions had human agents, a view Martin rejects. While the Pleistocene overkill hypothesis may be somewhat exaggerated, the apparent ease with which Paleo Indians could have killed animals by employing certain hunting techniques, combined with general environmental changes, could easily have led to the extermination of some species. But these extinctions probably did not occur within the space of a few years, or even decades, nor is it likely that prehistoric Indians were aware that they were happening. My archival data (1978) clearly indicate that it was not until the Northern Ojibwa had suffered extreme deprivation coupled with the repeated advice of sympathetic fur traders to alter their subsistence strategies that Indians gave up attempts to survive on the almost exterminated large animals. Thus, both Paleo Indians and the nineteenth-century Ojibwa appear to have been attempting to survive according to traditional methods which under altering environmental conditions were no longer viable. The view that the aboriginal Indian was a functional conservationist because he feared reprisal from animal spirits—if in fact this was really the case—may simply have been a metaphorical expression of an implicit view that waste was bad. Martin himself states that Indians had "a clear injunction against wasting game" (p. 83n). Further, even though this metaphor may have been phrased in terms of reprisal, it does not mean that Indians did not simultaneously love nature, whatever that may imply. Although the Indian view of nature was "an alien ideology of land-use" (p. 188) when compared to the Western view, I suggest that a key difference between the two systems was an absence in the former of a more general concept of animal population dynamics. And just as it is possible to practice conservation without "respecting" game, so it is possible to respect animals and simultaneously and perhaps unawaredly hunt them to extinction if the motives and means for obtaining them are present. What appears to Westerners as waste may not have been construed as such by Indians, and so it cannot simply be assumed that certain forms of behavior reflect something as vaguely defined as despiritualization. For example, is it necessarily wasteful for Indians to kill caribou for the hides only when they need winter clothing while the meat, which they do not require, is left to rot? (See Shepard Krech's argument in Chapter 5 for an elaboration on this point.)

If the traditional Indian did indeed "love" nature rather than fear it, or even if he both loved and feared it simultaneously, then he was more than a functional conservationist and so he may have something to tell the troubled ecologist. So might the historical Indian, whose survival strategies came to involve operating within bounded tracts of land and with deliberate conservation practices. The northeastern Indian view of nature, at least that part of it stressing the evils of waste, might be successfully employed by the ecology movement, especially when combined with our contemporary understanding of systems ecology. Nevertheless, since what seems to have been overexploitation to the ethnohistorian was not usually interpreted as such by most Indians in the fur trade who lacked this concept until after the fact, this portion of the Indian ideological system must be replaced by Western knowledge. The acceptance of the latter, however, does not rule out the former. Thus, rather than looking elsewhere for spiritual inspiration, the troubled ecologist should attempt to understand the Indian meaning of nature, especially as it applied to the fur trade context. Perhaps Martin should also make further attempts to do the same.

Note

I wish to thank my wife, M. Estellie Smith, for carefully reading this paper and for making suggestions to improve it. She cannot, however, be held responsible for any errors or the particular views expressed here. I wish also to express my gratitude to the Governor and Committee of the Hudson's Bay Company for permission to view their extensive archival materials, from which many of the ideas expressed in this paper were formed.

References Cited

Bishop, Charles A.
    1970   The Emergence of Hunting Territories among the
                Northern Ojibwa. Ethnology 9:1–15.
    1974   The Northern Ojibwa and the Fur Trade: An Histor-

ical and Ecological Study. Toronto: Holt, Rinehart &
Winston.

1978   Cultural and Biological Adaptations to Deprivation:
The Northern Ojibwa Case. *In* Extinction and
Survival in Human Populations, ed. Charles D.
Laughlin and Ivan A. Brady, pp. 208–30. New York:
Columbia University Press.

1979   Limiting Access to Limited Goods: The Origins of
Stratification in Interior British Columbia. Paper presented at the American Ethnological Society Meet-
ings, Vancouver, B.C., April 23–24, 1979. (To be
published in the Proceedings.)

1980   Kwah: A Carrier Chief. *In* Old Trails and New Di-
rections: Papers of the Third North American Fur
Trade Conference, ed. Carol M. Judd and Arthur J.
Ray, pp. 191–204. Toronto: University of Toronto
Press.

Bishop, Charles A., and Shepard Krech III

1980   Matriorganization: The Basis of Aboriginal Subarctic
Social Organization. Arctic Anthropology (in press).

Dailey, Robert C.

1968   The Role of Alcohol among North American Indian
Tribes as Reported in the Jesuit Relations. Anthropologica 9:45–59.

Harris, Marvin

1979   Cultural Materialism: The Struggle for a Science of
Culture. New York: Random House.

Hickerson, Harold

1960   The Feast of the Dead among the Seventeenth-
Century Algonkians of the Upper Great Lakes.
American Anthropologist 62:81–107.

1962   The Southwestern Chippewa: An Ethnohistorical
Study. American Anthropological Association
Memoir 92.

1963   The Sociohistorical Significance of Two Chippewa
Ceremonials. American Anthropologist 65:67–85.

1967   Some Implications of the Theory of Particularity, or

"Atomism," of Northern Algonkians. Current Anthropology 8:313–43.

1970   The Chippewa and Their Neighbors: A Study in Ethnohistory. New York: Holt, Rinehart and Winston.

1973   Fur Trade Colonialism and the North American Indian. Journal of Ethnic Studies 1:15–44.

Hockett, Charles F., and Robert Ascher

1964   The Human Revolution. Current Anthropology 5:135–68.

Leacock, Eleanor

1954   The Montagnais "Hunting Territory" and the Fur Trade. American Anthropological Association Memoir 78.

Martin, Calvin

1978   Keepers of the Game: Indian-Animal Relationships and the Fur Trade. Berkeley: University of California Press.

Ray Arthur J.

1974   Indians in the Fur Trade. Toronto: University of Toronto Press.

1978   History and Archaeology of the Northern Fur Trade. American Antiquity 43:26–34.

Ray, Arthur J., and Donald Freeman

1978   Give Us Good Measure: An Economic Analysis of Relations between the Indians and the Hudson's Bay Company before 1763. Toronto: University of Toronto Press.

Sahlins, Marshall

1972   Stone Age Economics. Chicago: Aldine.

Smith, Adam

1950   An Inquiry into the Nature and Causes of the Wealth of Nations (1776). 6th ed. 2 vols. London: Methuen.

CHAPTER FOUR

KEEPERS OF THE GAME AND THE NATURE OF EXPLANATION

DEAN R. SNOW

CALVIN MARTIN's hypothesis has been described as provocative on several occasions, as he perhaps intended it should. It has provoked symposia two years in a row (1978 and 1979), and for that we should thank him, for friendly controversy is the staple food of an organization like the American Society for Ethnohistory.

My own view of Martin's hypothesis is that at its current level of elaboration it remains too simplistic and too facile to cover the broad range of evidence he seeks to explain. I have no doubt that the underlying principles of sociocultural systems are quite simple, as fundamental principles always are, but these lie at a much deeper level than Martin's level of abstraction. On the level at which his hypothesis operates, sociocultural systems are very complex and rarely yield to straightforward cause-effect explanations. As someone named Anderson once said, "I have yet to see any problem, however complicated, which, when you looked at it in the right way, did not become still more complicated" (Dickson 1978:4). In light of this, I would like to point out some shortcomings in Martin's hypothesis and suggest ways in which we can correct those shortcomings by expanding and building upon it.

As it now stands, the hypothesis suffers from a few basic fallacies that are there primarily as a result of its simplicity. Central to these, of course, is the reductive fallacy, which reduces complexity to simplicity, or sometimes diversity to uniformity. David Fischer's (1970:172) favorite example is the war that was lost for want of a horseshoe nail. Lacking the nail the shoe was lost, causing the horse to be lost, causing the rider to be lost, causing the message to be lost, causing the loss of the regiment, the bat-

61

tle, and so on. As far as it has been developed to date, Martin's hypothesis is about at the lost rider level of abstraction. We cannot deny that he has found some basic evidence and made some valid inferences, about nails, horseshoes, and horses if you will. But despite the validity of those findings, the hypothesis is not yet sufficient to explain the large range of cases Martin treats. To belabor the analogy just a bit more, there are few if any wars whose outcomes were determined just by the loss of a single rider. Others have already pointed out analogous cases that cannot be made to fit Martin's hypothesis. Many aboriginal belief systems survived into the nineteenth century, even though the hypothesis predicts their earlier demise; in some cases epidemics occurred *after* the advent of the fur trade. These and other ill-fitting cases clearly require expansion and elaboration of the hypothesis.

Oversimplification has contributed to some additional fallacies. Martin (p. 12) discusses the "merits and demerits of the substantivist and formalist doctrines of economic anthropology" and subsequently adopts a substantivist view. It is my view that discussion in this subject has tended to become polarized to the point that we have been trapped by the fallacy of false dichotomy. This type of fallacy has reached almost epidemic proportions in both anthropology and historical research, and I suppose that Claude Lévi-Strauss would tell us that it is universally endemic given the innate dualism of human mentality. Certainly we cannot blame Calvin Martin for inventing it, yet it mars his work just the same.

A more serious criticism is the tendency toward rhetorical overstatement and the consequences that tendency has. We are told that what emerges from the ethnohistorical record is "the notion of a technologically incompetent, uninspired aborigine who was transformed into a highly efficient agent of wildlife destruction once he became equipped with a lethal technology and gained access to the European marketplace" (Martin 1978:9). While Martin might claim that this overstatement summarizes the views of others and not himself, it is nonetheless his own.

Martin seeks to discredit the conclusions of others, not by careful analysis, but by presenting them as caricatures, a device that is more appropriate in political than in academic argument. Forceful assertions are no substitute for good documentation. Yet in another place, Martin (p. 61) tells us that his concern is "less to document this transformation [in ideology] than to assess its impact on the Indian-land relationship." I would insist that ethnohistorians must do both, lest hypotheses come to stand in place of the documentation that might invalidate them. That, I fear, is what has happened in this case.

My own approach to cultural systems as recorded in either the ethnohistorical or the archaeological record has been to abstract them into economic, social, technological, and ideological (or religious) subsystems. I often break these into fourteen smaller categories in the manner indicated in Table 1.

The fourteen categories of Table 1, like the larger subsystems, are often not mutually exclusive, and I do not propose that they necessarily be given equal weight in subsequent analysis. Additional categories are possible if one drops the requirement that they must be archaeologically discoverable. The scheme is essentially a positivist one, and the objection can be (and has been) raised that the ideological subsystems of Native American cultural systems are undiscoverable by Western minds, that even the use of the word *ideological* skews the separate reality of Native American thought. This epistemological pessimism is usually expressed by those taking an idealist rather than a positivist position when examining ethnographic data. In its most extreme form, this position leads to the conclusion that Native American thought is undiscoverable by anyone operating within the Western scientific tradition. A less extreme view holds that ideology is itself a Western concept that cannot be imposed on Native American thought. In my view the first position is extremist nonsense. As for the less extreme criticism, I use *ideological* only to refer to that cultural subsystem pertaining to or concerned with ideas, a definition accepted by most English dictionaries. These points are important because Martin and I appear to share

Table 1. Cultural subsystems and fourteen attributes that can be drawn from either archaeological or ethnohistorical evidence.

ECONOMIC SUBSYSTEM
1. Site types and distribution within the area
2. House types and distribution within settlements
3. Food resources and seasonality
4. Seasonal movements

SOCIAL SUBSYSTEM
5. Household unit
6. Settlement unit
7. Other inferred institutions
8. Inferred community activities

TECHNOLOGICAL SUBSYSTEM
9. Artifact types
10. Trade goods
11. Raw materials
12. Specific activities

IDEOLOGICAL SUBSYSTEM
13. Mortuary site types
14. Burial programs

the view that ideology is discoverable. We differ in our assessments of the impact of ideological factors on other cultural subsystems. Thus the introduction of the more extreme idealist viewpoint into the symposium in which these papers were read served only to divert attention away from the main issue, and it is important for anyone reading this paper or any other contribution to this volume to be aware of the level at which the main issue is being debated.

Key factors in the Eastern Abenaki cultural system in Maine around A.D. 1610 included subsistence activities such as moose hunting, fishing, gathering, and other hunting-trapping activities. Maize horticulture was marginally important, and new factors, including the fur trade and the availability of European manufactured goods, were gaining a foothold. All of these factors influenced one another in a complex array of positive and negative feedback loops. The dependent variable of population was positively reinforced by most factors. The fur trade had a positive effect on maize horticulture because it provided the Abenaki with a hedge against years of crop failure, and they were able to risk more dependence upon corn than had been the case prehistorically. All of this was rationalized in a variety of ways by Abenaki ideology, and I see no evidence that outmoded ideology was in any way impacting adversely upon the system, although it probably acted as a restraint on rapid change.

By 1620, the Eastern Abenaki cultural system had to cope with the additional factors of intertribal warfare, settlement nucleation, and epidemics of European diseases. While the epidemics impacted very negatively on population, and doubtless impacted on all other factors as well one way or another, I see no evidence that it perverted information flow as such. Ideology can be viewed at least in part as the rationalization of the decision-making process that produces the positive and negative feedback loops between key elements in the cultural system. When we talk about ideology as a factor in and of itself in such a system, we usually mean those cultural features that assist in the organization and continuity of that rationalization process, not just the process itself. There are invariably anachronisms in the features of ideology and functional flaws in the rationalization process, but I have yet to see anything here or elsewhere in North American ethnohistory having the grotesque pathological dimensions proposed by Martin.

It seems clear to me that in most cultural systems most of the time, ideology has been largely a product of other factors and not itself a factor that significantly influenced other factors either positively or negatively. If ideology were added as a factor in the Eastern Abenaki case, what we know of Abenaki ethnohistory would require us to show most feedback loops pointing positive or negative arrows towards ideology, not out of it. Indeed, this is more often than not the case even in cultural systems that are documented only archaeologically. A good example is provided by the Moorehead complex, a prehistoric mortuary subsystem that lasted from about 3200 B.C. to 1800 B.C. in Maine and the Maritimes. I have concluded that caribou hunting, marine hunting, the use of dugout canoes, and a relatively dense population were positive reinforcements for this ideological subsystem and its physical trappings, and that its demise resulted from the demise of those reinforcing factors. Their demise was in each case the result of changes in still other factors. Caribou populations may have dwindled because of the advance of mixed forest and bog environments, with a consequent increase in the moose population. Marine hunting may well have died out as swordfish and other primary resources were reduced by changes in seawater temperature. New subsistence practices appear to have led to a shift from dugout to birchbark canoes, which in turn led to the gradual disappearance of gouges, adzes, and other heavy woodworking tools formerly used in dugout canoe manufacture. Because these tools and the slate-tipped spears used to hunt animals that had been previously central to subsistence all were disappearing from the inventory, and because they were also important as grave goods, it is no surprise that the mortuary subsystem underwent change. No doubt the ideology that helped to rationalize the changing system changed as well. While it might be tempting to assert that the Moorehead complex disappeared as the ultimate consequence of the growth of a mixed forest and bogs, such a cause-effect explanation is, under the circumstances, at least a gross oversimplification. It would be an even greater error to suggest that the changing ideological subsystem represented by the Moorehead complex was the prime mover in this broad systemic evolution, for it was quite clearly a dependent variable.

Thus, to return to the hypothesis at hand, while it is not impossible that ideology had some temporary role as a positive or negative factor influencing other factors in some specific cultural systems, it cannot serve as a prime mover in most specific instances or in the functioning of cultural systems generally. I do not deny that Martin may have found some specific cases where ideological change led to overhunting, but I do deny that this observation can be expanded to a hypothesis having general validity in northern North America after A.D. 1600. What is required is an expansion and elaboration of the hypothesis such that it includes as many additional factors as necessary to cover the specifics of systems that operated in separate regions and at separate times. For example, population declines pushed Indian communities far below earlier levels, changing the demographic equilibrium of the native systems, and in effect increasing the amount of game and other resources per person in a given region. At the same time permanent European communities and individual European hunters intruded into regions that had been previously beyond them, in effect making it impossible for Indians alone to manage the harvesting of game. These factors alone would lead rational people to pay less attention to balanced exploitation than previously, and they would not need the rhetoric of warfare against the animals as a rationale after the fact, much less a reason in and of itself.

Eastern Abenaki shamanism, as described by Eckstorm (1945) and Speck (1970) is complex, and a brief review of it shows how an historian might get the wrong idea. Common illnesses were thought to be curable by various herbal remedies which were administered by recognized curers. It is likely that the cures were thought to have powers beyond the purely biological ones credited to them by modern medical science, but their use was nonetheless not enmeshed in Abenaki shamanism. Shamans were seen as a class of very powerful people who were apart from the more visible and benign curers. They were often feared because of their power and because nonshamans were not fully aware of their identities. Shamans could cause illness and could effect cures by ceasing to cause it. In that sense only were they usually curers. They could transform themselves into animal forms and leave their unconscious human forms behind to roam about in those forms. Reference to these forms as animal helpers instead of the alternate forms the Abenaki conceived them to be appears to be the product of Western misunderstanding. The most powerful shamans had several animal forms, and their power expressed itself in terms of personal charisma, political power, and sexual potency as well. There are stories of hunters encountering animals fighting pitched battles with one another, or lone animals acting strangely, and these observations were commonly interpreted as shamans fighting one another in their animal forms or carrying out some other aggressive act while in animal form. One hunter reported hitting a strange fox in the shoulder with a rock, only to discover upon returning home that another man had an unexplained shoulder injury. The logic of Abenaki ideology led to the obvious conclusion that the injured man was a shaman and that the hunter had injured him while he was in his animal form. Thus Abenaki shamanism functioned to deflect hostility into the animal realm and out of human society. The aggressive impulses of strong personalities were vented through or against animal surrogates. If shamans were thought to cause some diseases, it is easy to see how an epidemic might raise anxiety and perhaps increase hostility toward animals suspected of being transformed shamans. But this would not really be evidence of war on animals as such. If animals caused disease, it was only those specific animals that were shamans in disguise that were the culprits, and it seems highly unlikely to me that the Eastern Abenaki would have extended their destructive rage to whole species.

In fact, the Eastern Abenaki appear never to have indulged in the ideologically-inspired overkill Martin's hypothesis predicts should have begun after the epidemics of the seventeenth century. As late as 1764, a century and a half after the most devastating epidemics, the Penobscot Indians were complaining that white hunters were overexploiting the beaver population and making it impossible for the Indians to manage the resource in such a way that a steady harvest could be maintained (Chadwick 1889). The Indians could not stop the overexploitation of their non-Indian competitors, and they were left with no choice but to join them in grabbing as much of the beaver resource as they could before it disappeared. The Penobscot fur trade declined for the rest of the century and was virtually dead by 1820.

Martin has himself pointed out some other additional factors that must be taken into account in an expanded analysis of evolving Native American cultural systems. For example, he notes that some tribes were not responsive to efforts by the Hudson Bay Company to increase the number of pelts traded by increasing the price paid (p. 10). Indeed, increased prices seemed to lead to decreased pelt supplies. Martin cites E. E. Rich's explanation that the Indians in this time and in this region still treated trade as a form of gift exchange, and the emphasis was still upon maintaining a constant flow of European goods. The observation makes very good sense to anyone familiar with Native American cultures. We can see strong archaeological evidence for gift exchange in the Adena-Hopewell trade networks of 2,000 years ago, and I am convinced that there is clear if somewhat rare evidence for it going back to the Paleo-Indian period, over 10,000 years ago.

So clearly, ideology does sometimes have a role to play in adaptation. Trade or anything else is in large measure what you perceive it to be, and if the Indians of a given cultural system perceived it to be gift exchange, then that perception influenced their behavior. Two more points flow from this observation. First, any ethnohistorical research must allow for known and probably cultural factors like but not limited to the one I just mentioned. Against this is a second point, namely that the influence of ideology is usually short-lived, for ideology is one of the most maleable of cultural subsystems. If something has to give in the system, ideology is an always-vulnerable option, even though people often succeed in altering this subsystem while seeming to fortify it. Nativistic movements are often much more selective than they pretend to be, and any number of examples of ideological expediency masquerading as hoary tradition can be pulled from recent political speeches. Even without adopting a decidedly materialist perspective it is hard to escape the conclusion that in most cultural systems ideology functions in the service of other less elastic needs. Only rarely does ideology become a dysfunctional prime mover. While it is remotely possible that Martin has found such a rare example, the evidence seems to say that he has not. The burden of proof clearly lies on Martin's hypothesis, and as presently stated it cannot support that burden.

The importance of Calvin Martin's work is that it pulls one such case from the ethnohistorical record and forces us to analyze it closely. The problem, however, is that the hypothesis applies in only some places and in those places explains a short-lived phenomenon at best. Martin has not yet gone far enough; the hypothesis remains too simple to explain adequately the evolution of complex social systems, and too complicated to be an underlying principle of Native American social organization. I hope that we can expect much more on this and related subjects from Calvin Martin, for there is clearly much work to be done and too few scholars ready to do it. Anthropologists will continue to drive historians crazy with their sloppy source criticism and other technical failings. Historians will continue to drive anthropologists crazy with notions of cause and effect that seem to lie outside the bounds of known human behavior. But out of this collective madness comes scholarship that is much better stuff than it could ever be if we stayed behind our disciplinary fences.

References Cited

Chadwick, Joseph
    1889   An Account of a Journey from Fort Pownal—now Fort Point—up the Penobscot River to Quebec, in 1764. Bangor Historical Magazine 4:141–48.

Dickson, Paul
   1978   The Official Rules. New York: Delacorte.
Eckstorm, Fannie Hardy
   1945   Old John Neptune and Other Maine Indian Sha-
            mans. Portland: Southworth-Anthoensen.
Fischer, David H.
   1970   Historians' Fallacies. New York: Harper & Row.
Martin, Calvin
   1978   Keepers of the Game: Indian-Animal Relationships
            and the Fur Trade. Berkeley: University of California
            Press.
Speck, Frank G.
   1970   Penobscot Man. New York: Octagon Books.

CHAPTER FIVE

"THROWING BAD MEDICINE": SORCERY, DISEASE, AND THE FUR TRADE AMONG THE KUTCHIN AND OTHER NORTHERN ATHAPASKANS

SHEPARD KRECH III

NORTHERN ATHAPASKANS, hunter-fishers of the western Subarctic, participated in the European fur trade from its inception. They traded both meat and furs, often with great enthusiasm and trapping out some animal populations in the process, in exchange for metal and cloth goods, beads, tobacco, and up to a time, alcohol. Northern Athapaskans also succumbed, sometimes in substantial numbers, to diseases introduced by whites or by other Indian groups.

Why did they participate with such gusto in the trade? In *Keepers of the Game*, Calvin Martin suggests that the complex of disease, taboo violations, and a retaliation of extermination proposed for the eastern Subarctic Micmac and Ojibwa was found elsewhere: the eastern Subarctic "grim tale was to be repeated many times along the moving Indian-white frontier" (p. 65). "In Eastern Canada, anyway, and quite possibly in other areas of the continent where the trade was prosecuted with comparable vigor, a long-standing compact between the animal kingdom and man was evidently disrupted; the mutual obligation–mutual courtesy relationship was dissolved, first as a result of the spiritually disintegrative effects of exotic diseases and, later on, Christian proselytization and the trade itself" (pp. 184–85).

Northern Athapaskans offer an ideal test of the extension of Martin's thesis, because, like eastern Subarctic Indians, their participation in the trade was, though variable, at times highly vigorous; they suffered from epidemic diseases; and their knowledge of and intimacy with animals was profound, since they depended on them (and fish) for their livelihood. The aim of this chapter, then, is to evaluate the extension of Martin's hypothesis to Northern Athapaskans. This will be done in three stages: first, through a detailed examination of data from the Kutchin, the Northern Athapaskans with whom I am most familiar; next, by focusing on the Chipewyan and Koyukon, two Athapaskan groups mentioned by Martin; and finally, by a broader comparative consideration of Northern Athapaskan disease etiology. The emphasis throughout is placed, where possible, on the earliest phases of contact, which for the Kutchin came in the last decade of the eighteenth and first half of the nineteenth centuries, when they became involved in an exchange with Euro-Canadian fur traders but had not yet been exposed to the message of Anglican and Oblate missionaries.

The Early Historic Kutchin, 1789–1860

The aboriginal, or prehistoric, era ended and the stage of indirect contact, or the protohistoric period—marked by the indirect dissemination of trade goods, of knowledge of whites, and perhaps of diseases (Bishop and Ray 1976:64)—began for bands of eastern Kutchin at some point during the decades 1750–89. The exact timing of this is uncertain. Direct contact, or the historic period, arrived during the years 1789–1804: in 1789 the Kutchin were first contacted by Alexander Mackenzie on his exploratory voyage to the Arctic Ocean and in 1804, either the North West or XY Company established Fort Good Hope in the territory of the Hare, Athapaskans located immediately southeast of the Kutchin. The extent of contact between 1789 and 1804 is unknown, although at least one voyage to the Mackenzie Delta, through eastern Kutchin territory, was made: in the summer of 1799, a Euro-Canadian trader was killed by Mackenzie Eskimos (Anon. 1822) and before his demise he may have encountered Kutchin camped along the Mackenzie. From 1823 to 1827, Fort Good Hope was located 100 miles further down the Mackenzie

River, close to trading and fishing locales favored by Kutchin (Franklin 1828:40). In the 1840s, two Hudson's Bay Company posts—Peel River Post (1840) and Fort Yukon (1847)—were established in Kutchin territory.

Knowledge of the Kutchin prior to the 1821 amalgamation of the North West and Hudson's Bay companies is scanty. This period was certainly important for the establishment of trading relationships, and it may also have been for the transmission of diseases. In the late 1790s, there was one North West Company post along the Mackenzie (130 km. from Great Slave Lake), and in the period 1804–15, posts were operated at Fort Good Hope, Great Bear Lake, The Forks (Fort Simpson), and Fort Norman. Competition between the XY and North West companies erupted at Great Bear Lake prior to their amalgamation in 1804 and may have affected the Kutchin (Cooke and Holland 1971).

The Trade

The few glimpses we have of the Kutchin before 1820 stress their commercial tendencies. In 1806, some Kutchin traded beaver and marten pelts for ironwork and beads. Guns were not traded at this time, and the Kutchin "hoped that the Eskimaux would not come to attack them" (McKenzie 1805–6:25).

Apparently, beads and dentalia were highly desired by the Kutchin from the very outset of the Euro-Canadian trade, and this may have been a reflection of aboriginal values (see Osgood 1971:128). In 1814, eastern Kutchin trading at Fort Good Hope were "near creating an uproar on account of a deficiency of beads at the Fort. For two successive years a pressing demand had been made for beads, it being well understood that the Loucheux tribe would scarcely trade anything else, and for the want of this, their favorite article, they preferred taking back to their tents the peltries they had brought to trade" (Wentzel 1889–90:110). Before 1820, beads were used for decoration, strung on sinew and tied to one's hair or clothing (McKenzie 1805:27). In trade with Eskimos, Kutchin "obtain[ed], at a high price, certain smooth sea-shells, to be inserted as ornaments into the septum of the nose" (Anon. 1822:19). This interethnic trade was probably ancient, since, at the beginning of the historic period, some Kutchin had a bow and iron objects obtained in trade from Eskimos (Mackenzie 1970:190–212 passim), and Kutchin and Inuit traditions and archaeological and ethnohistorical evidence support the existence of an aboriginal trading relationship (see Krech 1979b).

In the 1830s, the Kutchin continued to press for beads, and hesitated to trade their furs at Fort Good Hope for beads that were small or of poor quality (HBCA B.80/a/7–14 passim). In 1831, some Kutchin, "so often disappointed in the article of beads for three or four years past," were not going to travel to Fort Good Hope, and the Hudson's Bay Company traders, viewing the loss of their trade as a "great drawback on the usual returns," traveled to Kutchin territory and showed them beads which they hoped would convince them to continue to patronize Fort Good Hope (HBCA B.80/a/9–10). Although after 1821 the Mackenzie Drainage was a monopoly trade area, western Kutchin had another option for trade in Russian traders in southeastern and western Alaska. Russian goods—primarily beads, knives, and other metal items—reached the Kutchin during the first quarter of the nineteenth century (Krech 1976).

Beads and dentalia shells continued to be key items in the trade throughout the first half of the nineteenth century. By mid-century, beads were a general-purpose money: they were used as an exchange standard, with a specific bead-string length considered equivalent to the Made Beaver, the Hudson's Bay Company standard; they were used to pay for furs, moose skins, a shaman's services; and they were used to evaluate wealth. Beads also were distributed after a death, and they continued to be used extensively as decoration (Franklin 1828:43; Hardisty 1872:311–19; Jones 1872:320–25; Kirby 1872:418; Murray 1910: 84–90; Richardson 1851, 1:380–81, 391; Simpson 1843:190).

Guns were traded to the Kutchin by the 1820s (Krech 1979b) and became important trade items, in part because of the hostile relationship between Kutchin and Eskimos. During the 1820s and 1830s, Kutchin took great quantities of ammunition for defense against the Eskimos (Krech 1979*b*). And until shortly after mid-century, the eastern Kutchin controlled the access of Eskimos to Hudson's Bay Company posts, a control possible because of their possession of guns. The Eskimos were contemptuous of the Kutchin (and other neighboring Athapaskans) who did not have guns.

It was also Hudson's Bay Company policy to exchange ammunition for provisions and encourage a provision trade, although this sometimes interfered with the flow of furs. In the 1830s, the traders advised the Indians that it was "injunctive to be more industrious in hunting furs . . . those who did not bring some furs, need not come merely to trade provisions" (HBCA B.80/a/7/fo. 1). In the 1840s and 1850s, though, Kutchin brought provisions (sorely needed by the traders) on one-half of their trading trips (Krech 1976), along with many furs. In the 1830s, the upper reaches of the Arctic Red River were "ruined of Beaver" by the Kutchin (HBCA B.80/a/10/fo. 9d), and the Hudson's Bay Company cast its eyes toward the Peel River, a known rich source of furs (HBCA B.80/a/7/fo. 3d; Isbister 1845:355; Simpson 1843:186).

Although guns and ammunition were popular trade items, whether guns were effective, particularly in hunting, is problematic. In 1825, one man "out hunting saw 2 Rein Deer but unfortunately his gun would not make fire. These guns are very subject to freezing, particularly Wilsons Guns of which the Indians complain very much" (HBCA B.80/a/4/fo. 6). Guns were used in combination with aboriginal surround and barrier techniques. By mid-century, guns were in strong demand throughout the Kutchin area. Their important use in intertribal (Kutchin-Inuit) relations has already been referred to. In addition, guns were highly desired in intraband relationships, as prestige items. Those who did not carry these costly items (at a price of 20 Made Beaver, the most expensive item in the Hudson's Bay Company inventory) traded nonetheless for powder and ball which they would exchange, in turn, with gun carriers for a share of meat (Murray 1910:85; see Isbister 1845:338). Throughout the first half of the nineteenth century, Kutchin in strategically located territories were quick to seize mercantilist opportunities, becoming traders following the establishment of trading posts. In the 1820s and 1830s, Kutchin living along the Mackenzie traded for the furs of more distant bands at a river nine days from the upstream location of Fort Good Hope. Some Kutchin quickly became middlemen in the Eskimo-Hudson's Bay Company trade (Franklin 1828:99–109, 195–97). In the 1840s, the Upper Porcupine River Kutchin assumed a lucrative middleman position in the Peel River Post trade, and more distant Kutchin traded to them one-half again as many furs as they would have to trade in order to receive the same goods at Peel River Post. During the same period the Peel River Kutchin were receiving twice as many furs from more distant groups as the company would have received. The 1847 establishment of Fort Yukon in western Kutchin territory undermined the Upper Porcupine Kutchin trade and "enraged" them, according to one trader. The Yukon Flats Kutchin, in whose territory Fort Yukon was built, became highly aggressive traders and by the mid 1860s, hunted very little for themselves, depending instead on barter for their subsistence goods. The Yukon Flats Kutchin interfered so much in the trade that the Hudson's Bay Company considered moving the post (see Krech 1976).

Thus, by the late 1830s, the Kutchin were deeply involved in the trade—whether in provisions or in furs is quite beside the point—and middleman positions and the importance they attached to beads reflected their mercantilist tendencies. They welcomed the 1840 extension of the trade to Peel River Post: informed of the company decision, "Such was the joy this intimation infused among them, that a Dance was immediately set up, in which they all joined with more than usual hilarity" (HBCA B.80/a/15/fo. 5d).

Beads, dentalia, and guns were the most important trade items throughout the first half of the nineteenth century, when A. H. Murray's (1910:100) comment "Guns and beads, beads and guns is all the cry in our country" prevailed. The Kutchin demand for goods was strong, they exchanged large numbers of marten, beaver, and muskrat, and they were aggressive traders. Mercantilist-minded, they appreciated the material dimensions of the exchange.

Might epidemic diseases have preceded their enthusiasm? Might there have been some renunciation of aboriginal belief that freed the Kutchin to participate with such evident enthusiasm in the trade? I turn now to a consideration of these questions.

Diseases

There is no evidence that any epidemic disease reached the Kutchin during the indirect-contact protohistoric period or during the historic period prior to the 1820s. In 1789, Alexander Mackenzie remarked that a Hare woman had "an Abscess in the Belly and is reduced to a mere Skeleton" (1970:191); he considered Slavey to be "an ugly meagre ill made People particularly about the Legs which are very clumsy and full of Scabs. . . . Many of them appear'd very sickly" (1970:183), and he attributed the scabs to sitting too close to fires and the sickly appearance to a "Dirty" life; but Mackenzie Flats Kutchin appeared "healthy and full of Flesh and more cleanly" than other Indians (1970:192).

In contrast, in the mid-1820s and again in the middle and late 1830s, all groups trading at Fort Good Hope were ravaged by disease. In the mid-1820s, Kutchin and Hare were dying from a "dreadful sickness," a "contagious distemper" that killed adults and children. "Mortality so prevalent" caused a decline in the trade (HBCA B.80/a/4–5; see Franklin 1828:41). In the mid-1830s, Hare and Kutchin again were sick and dying from "the disease so prevalent among them" (HBCA B.80/a/11/fo. 13).

The early 1840s, early 1850s, and mid-1860s were no less severe. In 1843, Peel River Kutchin suffered from a "very bad cough . . . from which children were cut off" (HBCA B.157/a/3/fo. 12d); in the mid-1840s many Han women in a group in trading

81

contact with the Kutchin died (Murray 1910:69). In 1851–52, eastern Kutchin were sick; deaths peaked during the spring of 1852, when the Hudson's Bay Company clerk at Peel River Post remarked: "It is astonishing how rapidly the Indians are dying off" (Peers 5/10/1852). "A great many Indians" died during the next eighteen months (Anderson 11/24/1853). In the 1860s, scarlet fever devastated western Kutchin bands, obliterating one completely, and may have caused the death of from 10 to 33 percent of eastern Kutchin bands (see Krech 1978, 1979a).

In other words, on several occasions during the decades from 1820 to 1860, epidemic diseases ravaged Kutchin groups. But to what did the Kutchin attribute their illnesses?

Kutchin Explanations of Disease

The nineteenth-century Kutchin blamed sorcerers for sickness, disease, and death. There is no indication that they believed that offended animal spirits, outside of their operation through alliance with a shaman, could cause sickness. Shamans derived their power from animal-spirit helpers who came to them in dreams (Osgood 1936:155–56). In the early twentieth century, Kutchin believed that to violate any one of a large number of taboos on the use and care of animals risked offending the spirit of the animal and could cause bad luck that seemed to manifest itself primarily in a scarcity of animals (McKennan 1965:84).

Nineteenth-century Kutchin shamans foretold starvation, the success of hunting, and other events; they made wind in order to hunt moose; they cured diseases by singing, by phlebotomy, or by sucking and extracting a foreign object; and they both blamed distant sorcerers or shamans for sickness and could themselves exact revenge by sorcery. By the early twentieth century (if not before), spirit loss also was believed to cause sickness. (Jones 1872:325; Hardisty 1872:316–17; cf. McKennan 1965:77–79; Osgood 1936:156, 159.)

This belief system obtained throughout the first half of the nineteenth century, when Kutchin were devastated by epidemics and when Indians and Euro-Canadians alike were identified as sorcerers. One Hudson's Bay Company observer remarked just after mid-century: "It is when sickness prevails that the conjuror reigns supreme" (Hardisty 1872:316); in the 1850s, another trader commented: "No Indian dies a natural death, but is killed by the conjurations of another at some distance, and this supersition is the cause of much bloodshed among them" (Ross 1858).

In the 1840s, A. H. Murray reported that many Han, neighbors of the Kutchin, had died and many others were sick. The Han said that a Kutchin from whose band they had stolen a woman was responsible: "They believe that 'Vandeh' our hunter, to revenge the loss of said woman who was a relative of his, had made *medicine* to kill them, and now they wished to kill him that no more of their wives might die" (Murray 1910:51). Murray also commented of western Kutchin (and others) that "all tribes in this part of the country believe as gospel, that certain individuals have necromantic powers to cause the death of others, though a great distance apart" (Murray 1910:51). Euro-Canadians were not exempt from blame: Murray reported that after "the sudden death of a woman, wife to one of our principal men . . . it was at first believed that we were the cause of her death, but this was overruled and the blame attached to the lower band who had some disagreement with her husband" (1910:87; cf. Richardson 1851, 1:386). The Russians, trading farther west along the Yukon River, tried to take advantage of this belief in sorcery, and told Yukon Indians to say to the Han and Kutchin that "it was on account of our [the Hudson's Bay Company] being there in their country that so many of them had died in summer, that we were bad people" (Murray 1910:69).

The earliest evidence for this tendency of the Kutchin to blame whites for illness comes from Fort Good Hope in the disease-ravaged 1820s, when some Kutchin reported the imminent death of a leader in their band. John Bell, the Hudson's Bay Company clerk, remarked: "According to Indian supersititon [they] did not hesitate to say that I was the cause of his sickness by throwing bad Medicine upon him! on consequence of his sons having destroyed the boat left by Capt. Franklin and Party last fall below Red River. So much for Savage Supersititon!" (HBCA B.80/a/5/fo. 20).

In sum, the Kutchin were opportunists in the trade—coming often, eagerly, and from the start to obtain beads and guns, setting up highly evaluated middleman networks in which profits were substantial, and trapping out some animal populations; they were subject to a series of devastating epidemics, in which a number of them died; and, from all the available evidence, they tended to blame sorcerers for their sicknesses.

The Chipewyan and the Koyukon

How did other Northern Athapaskan groups compare with the Kutchin, especially with the Kutchin tendency to blame sorcerers, not animals, for illness?

The Athapaskan groups mentioned most often in *Keepers of the Game* are the Chipewyan and Koyukon. Martin suggests that the Chipewyan shared a similar belief system with the Cree and Ojibwa, that there were a number of "superstitions" related to catching fish, that game were to be treated with respect, that their "waste" of caribou was postcontact, and that they were despiritualized by the time of Hearne's lafe-eighteenth-century trek through their lands (pp. 71, 76–77, 109, 114, 145, 165). Martin states (p. 83), following Sullivan (1942:75–76), that the Koyukon regarded the slaughter of caribou with guns as a violation of the canon that "the Supreme Being punishes waste," and hence, it seems that we have both "waste" connected with the postcontact use of guns and the violation of various taboos linked with illness (pp. 63, 114, 126).

Does this evidence bear scrutiny?

The Chipewyan

Chipewyan participation in the fur trade is not easily sum-
marized. Chipewyan were first contacted by traders in the late
seventeenth century (Gillespie 1975*b*) and had started to bring
furs to Fort Churchill by 1719. Within two years, they brought
correctly dressed marten and beaver, an adaptation to trapping
termed "very rapid" (Gillespie 1975*b*:364). Yet, throughout the
first half of the eighteenth century, the needs of some Chipewyan
were limited to a few iron goods; thus, some brought few furs,
preferring instead to remain in their traditional ecological zone,
where caribou were abundant but beaver scarce (Gillespie 1975*b*:
366–68). Some traders reported their difficulty in inducing certain Chipewyan to trade furs (Gillespie 1975*a*, 1976). There was,
however, a substantial trade in provisions, and Dogrib and Yellowknives traded a great deal of caribou at Fort Providence in
the early nineteenth century (Gillespie 1975*a*:229). Although
beyond the scope of this essay, it would be of great interest to
examine the extent of the caribou meat and hide trade, since
this animal was symbolically important to the Chipewyan.

The Chipewyan and other Arctic Drainage Lowlands Athapaskans were affected by epidemic diseases in the late eighteenth and especially the early nineteenth centuries, but like the
Kutchin, they tended to blame sorcerers for these diseases.

Epidemic diseases were particularly prevalent among Arctic
Drainage Lowlands Athapaskans during the first half of the
nineteenth century (Krech 1980), first in the years 1805–8 (Wentzel 1805–6, 1889–90:95; Keith 1889–90:79), then in 1819–23. In
the latter period, measles and dysentery were said to have "carried off one-third of the Indians in these parts" (Franklin 1823:
137; cf. Rich 1938:61, 81; HBCA B.181/a/2–4). These diseases
affected Chipewyan, as did others in the mid-1830s (Back
1936:187, 457).

By this time, some Chipewyan recognized that humans were
disease carriers: in 1819–20, Chipewyan fled sick Cree, apparently recognizing that they could contract disease from them

(Smith 1976:80), and in 1833, Chipewyan heard of a cholera epidemic in Montreal and asked for large debt in order to go as far away as possible for a year (Parker 1972:52). This recognition may have existed even earlier, for in 1781–82, during a smallpox outbreak, Chipewyan avoided Hudson's Bay Company traders, although it is uncertain whether they associated the disease specifically with Cree or Euro-Canadian carriers (Gillespie 1975a:207).

Chipewyan also blamed sorcerers. In 1769, several Chipewyan were ready to go to war against the Inuit, and "the reason they gave for it they have had Many of the Northern Indians died, and thay think the Usquemay have Cungered them to dith" (HBCA B.42/a/74/fo. 23d, in Smith and Burch 1979:82). In the late eighteenth century, Hearne reported that "when any of the principal Northern Indians die, it is generally believed that they are conjured to death, either by some of their own countrymen, by some of the Southern Indians, or by some of the Esquimaux" (1958:216–17). In addition to Southern Indians (Cree; see Birket-Smith 1930:82) and Eskimos, Europeans also were believed to cause sickness by "juggling" (Jenness 1956:18).

Sorcery also affected the availability of game and hunting success. In the early nineteenth century, some unsuccessful Fort Wedderburn hunters were "possessed" by an idea" that the N. W. [North West Company] have 'thrown bad medicine upon them' which no arguement can subvert" (Rich 1938:178).

Although sorcerers seem to have been a principal cause of sickness, and of some other misfortunes, this does not mean that the relationship between humans and animals was unimportant. To the contrary, the Chipewyan believed that humans and animals have souls, that in the mythic past the boundary between men and animals was indistinct if not absent, and that one must take special care in order not to offend animals. A lapse in care did not seem to cause sickness, however; rather, it affected how readily animals would allow hunters access to them. Thus, killing a caribou with a stick was regarded as not treating caribou well, as an infraction of a taboo, and might result in a scarcity of animals (see Birket-Smith 1930:79–81), a belief shared by the Dogrib (Mason 1946:17) and the Slavey. The Slavey say in addition that a man who clubbed a trapped animal would receive bad luck (MacNeish 1954:189). In 1833, when caribou remained far off on the barren lands, Yellowknives blamed a Chipewyan man who was said to have clubbed one animal—after they first blamed George Back's hidden meteorological instruments (Back 1836:203, 211–16). In recent decades, Chipewyan have blamed the Canadian Wildlife Service's capture and trapping program for a decline in the numbers of caribou, apparently believing that the mistreated spirits of tagged caribou warn other animals away from the region (Smith 1978:72).

The relationship between humans and caribou is particularly noteworthy, since "hunting caribou is the proper activity for a man and caribou are his proper food" (Sharp 1977:35), an importance attested to by a number of observers. Yet, as Hearne noticed on numerous occasions, the eighteenth-century Chipewyan seemed not to be conservation-minded, killing many caribou simply for the tongues and leaving carcasses to rot. Perhaps this was because, as J. G. E. Smith has remarked, Chipewyan "took caribou for granted as an unchanging resource to which little thought had to be given" (Smith 1975:406). Or perhaps our notion of what is or is not conservation-minded does not fit with eighteenth-century Chipewyan ideas. For them, mistreating caribou evidently was not extended from clubbing these important animals to leaving carcasses to rot; and mistreatment by clubbing affected only the future availability of caribou. I return to this issue in the final section of this essay.

The relationship between humans and animals is important in another way: dreams with (almost any) animal spirit establish a relationship with a guardian spirit. The spirit reveals "enabling knowledge," and a person with *inkonze* ("to know something a little") can then use this supernatural power to foretell events or to reveal the cause of illness (Smith 1973:8; cf. MacNeish 1954:191 on similar beliefs among the Slavey). The twentieth-century Chipewyan said that a person with enabling knowledge might reveal as causes of illness a wish for an incestuous relationship or crossing the path of a menstruating woman, although the latter usually meant bad luck in hunting (Smith 1973:13; cf. Mac-Neish 1954:188 on the Slavey). But the cause was also likely to be somebody else with *inkonze*, either another Chipewyan using *inkonze* against those deviating from societal norms as a means of social control or a Dogrib or Slavey using *inkonze* because a Chipewyan yearned for his wife (Smith 1973:14). *Inkonze* can be used to make people sick, to kill people, to kill dogs, to help starving people, and to send bad luck in hunting. Roots and herbs, a medicine bag and songs, may all be involved in using *inkonze*, as in 1906, when Chipewyan attempted to "kill [Cree by their] own roots" (Smith 1973:14–15). The use of roots and songs is of Cree derivation (ibid.:21), as is the belief that a devil or Bad Manitou can make one sick (Jenness 1956:18).

In sum, enabling knowledge can be and is used for malevolent ends, including sickness, and Chipewyan and other Arctic Drainage Lowlands Athapaskans ascribed sickness to the actions of sorcerers in the late eighteenth, the nineteenth, and the early twentieth centuries.

There is no evidence that animals were held responsible for epidemic diseases, although obviously, contact with animal spirits was a necessary prelude to the malevolent use of *inkonze*. Nor did there appear to be a tendency to avoid contact with diseased animals. In 1807, Wentzel reported that Slavey (?) "eat with as good appetite as if it was the most delicious food, any animal that they find that died either of wounds or sickness and which is already wasted by maggots" (1889–90:85). The previous year, there had been a "distemper" that killed off many animals (Wentzel 1805–6).

The Koyukon

For ethnographic information on the Koyukon, Martin depends on the field research of Robert J. Sullivan (1942), who spent one-half year among the Lower Koyukon in the mid-1930s. Sullivan reported a declining belief in powerful animal spirits, or *yega*, but an apparent continuing connection between taboo violation and explanations for misfortune: specifically (and of immediate interest for Martin's thesis), a Koyukon who claimed a caribou that he did not kill risked the death of one of his children, or one who did not punch out a bear's eyes risked blindness of one of his children; one who violated marten or wolverine taboos predisposed his own death, or the death of a relative or of yet unborn children; and to violate a beaver taboo meant possible sickness (Sullivan 1942:78, 86, 94, 103–4, 108). The Koyukon believed also that taboo violations made mink, otter, lynx, or beaver scarce (ibid.:94, 95, 99, 108).

Annette McFadyen Clark, who conducted fieldwork among the Koyukuk River Koyukon in the 1960s and 1970s, provides support for some of Sullivan's observations. Clark points out that the animate and inanimate world of the Koyukon is filled with spirits which have the potential to cause misfortune and which people must appease in order not to be harmed. Bear spirits are particularly dangerous, and improper treatment can make women sterile or men physically weak, or cause rheumatism and/or starvation in both sexes (Clark 1970:80–84). Clark adds that "one must treat with respect and proper ritual all food and fur-bearing forms in order not to offend, and in fact to appease, the animals' spirits or souls. If they are not correctly treated, they may decide a particular area is a bad place to live and thus will not be reborn there or be caught again, or they may cause various illnesses, including epilepsy, to befall the hunter and his family" (1970:85–86). The Koyukon believe also that humans have two souls, one of which shamans or spirits can take and harm, the other of which remains in the body until death, after which time it can cause harm (1970:81).

There are other reports of the Koyukon, most notably those of the Jesuit Julius Jetté, whose lengthy studies antedated Sullivan's by several decades. Jetté said that "medicine-men," or shamans, control spirits "which are good or bad at the will of their man-superior, serving him as well to harm others, by causing disease, misfortune or ill luck, as to benefit them, by curing disease, bringing prosperity and good luck" (1911:102). There are a number of spirits, mainly "fierce and cruel," including one whose "occupation . . . is to spread disease" (pp. 97, 99). The point is that shamans, who first dream and then in a solitary wandering see a blue flame and an amulet and acquire power (Jetté 1907:165), can control the spirits.

Sickness or disease was caused by animal protecting spirits, or *yega*. Inhering in each animal (including humans), in some plants, and in some inanimate objects is a *yega*, a "protecting spirit, jealous and revengeful, whose mission is not to avert harm from the person or thing which it protects but to punish the ones who harm or misuse it, and to visit them with the calamities most dreaded by the Ten'a: sickness and death of the offender, or of his near relatives" (Jetté 1911:101–2). Diseases were apparently ascribed also to omens: the appearance of a marmot, of a swarm of a particular small beetle, or of a yelping fox are omens of death, and in 1900 epidemics were "credited" by Koyukon to the appearance of a marmot (Jetté 1911:246).

The Koyukon evidently distinguished sickness or death that affected just one person or several people from epidemic diseases affecting many in a community. After Russian traders contacted Koyukon in 1838, the Koyukon were affected by diseases through the rest of the nineteenth century. In the period between the first visit of Malakof in 1838 and the 1842 trip of Zagoskin, there was an estimated 75 percent decline in the population of villages between Norton Sound and Nulato and many recent deaths above Nulato (Zagoskin, in Clark 1974:106–7). In 1843, the Koyukuk River Koyukon suffered in another epidemic (Michael 1967:146). In 1883, some "sickness" killed many of the Koyukon (Clark 1974:107). In 1901, one second-hand report suggested periodic epidemics of smallpox and scarlet fever in the nineteenth century that were "at times so violent that whole villages would be wiped out and districts almost depopulated" (Cantwell 1902:218).

Could this be connected to animal "waste"? Although Sullivan called the Great Being the "Giver of Food and The Avenger of Waste" (1942:20), Jetté reported of bear, beaver, caribou, moose, otter, marten, lynx, and wolverine: "As most of these animals are killed, either for their flesh or for their fur, the *yega* cannot be expected to avenge their death: if it did, the Ten'a could not live. No fear of killing too many is entertained, for the Ten'a hold that no animal species endowed with a *yega* can become extinct. . . . But what the *yega* prosecutes is the irreverent disposal of the bones or carcasses, the stealing of an animal caught in another man's trap, or similar prejudicial actions" (1911:604). The adults who are responsible or their children are afflicted with epilepsy (in the case of a stolen caribou), sore eyes (a stolen marten), rheumatism, or "incurable diseases." Alternatively, animals will not come to traps (1911:604–9). All misfortune, concluded Jetté, is ultimately traceable to shamans, whose main preoccupation was to bring disease (1911:718–20).

Jetté's observations seem borne out by the sparse historical evidence on epidemics and the causes assigned to them by the Koyukon. For example, in the early 1840s, when Zagoskin traveled up the Yukon River, some Koyukuk River Koyukon were dying, and the trip was thought to be risky, for "the terrible effects of the smallpox epidemic, which was supposed to have been introduced by the Russians, were fresh in the memory of everyone" (Michael 1967:146). The Koyukon blamed the Russians for this epidemic (which at Nulato peaked in 1839), though whether as sorcerers or not is unclear. In 1867, pleurisy struck the Koyukon, who "accused the Russians of having caused the sickness and death by their sorceries" (Dall 1870:193).

Other Northern Athapaskans

The tendency for Kutchin, Chipewyan, and Koyukon to blame sorcerers for disease was widespread among Arctic Drainage Lowlands and Cordilleran Athapaskans.[1] For example, the mid-nineteenth-century Hare and Dogrib believed "in the power of the Eskimos and of strange Indians to hurt them by incantations, or 'bad medicine'" (Richardson 1851, 2:22). This belief persisted into the early twentieth century, when the Dogrib (and Slavey and Yellowknives) regarded "personal enmity [as] the only cause of sickness" (Mason 1946:32).

In the early nineteenth century, Mackenzie Drainage Lowlands Slavey "generally attribute[d] particular events, such as death and other casualties, to their enemies, whom they consider[ed] likewise as the authors of eclipses and other phenomena" (Keith 1889–90:89; cf. Honigmann 1946:77). Shamans cured by singing, sucking, and extracting various objects; phlebotomy also was practiced (ibid.). Among the Fort Nelson Slavey, sorcerers could be members of one's own band but were more likely to be Kaska, "bad people" living to the west; and the Slavey were careful to hide their food, clothing, and hearth ashes whenever the Kaska were around so that the latter could not use these items in sorcery (Honigmann 1946:79).

The Cordilleran Kaska ascribed illness to the actions of sorcerers or witches who stole the mind or soul of an enemy. By the late nineteenth and early twentieth centuries, dysentery and other sicknesses were blamed on sorcerers, and children were identified as witch-scapegoats on several occasions (Honigmann 1947, 1970).[2] The Kaska also believed that the violation of a taboo could cause sickness; specifically, killing an otter, mink, or frog or toad or clubbing a wounded caribou might cause sickness or death (Honigmann 1964:108–14, 125; 1970:225).

Cordilleran groups other than the Kutchin and Kaska shared the belief in sorcery. The belief system of the Han was similar to that of the Kutchin. They believed that shamans derived their power from animal-spirit helpers who appeared in dreams, and that, with the aid of their helpers, they could ensure hunting success, stave off starvation, heal sick people by singing, extract or blow away sickness introjected by another shaman, and make someone sick or die by causing weasel or marten skins, small bones, roots, or other objects to enter their victim's body (Schmitter 1910:17–19). In the nineteenth and twentieth centuries, the Han ascribed sickness to the actions of sorcerers. In the 1840s, a Han leader died suddenly, and both Yukon Flats Kutchin sorcery and "the presence of White people in the country" (Richardson 1851, 1:396) were said to be the causes. An outbreak of disease, perhaps smallpox, in the 1860s that affected 500 Han and killed many and an 1897 epidemic of coughing and bleeding from the lungs both were said to have been caused supernaturally: "The Indians think that each of these epidemics was due to a bad medicine-man from elsewhere sending an evil spirit amongst them. The evil spirit was supposed to enter the man's body in the form of an animal and, by moving about in him, produced sickness" (Schmitter 1910:17). And in the early twentieth century one man with tuberculosis and complications said that a Tanana shaman sent an eagle quill into his body and made him sick (Schmitter 1910:19).

The finest study of a Cordilleran group is that of the Southern Tutchone (and Tagish and Inland Tlingit) by Catharine McClellan. McClellan comments: "From the time he 'came to his senses' until he died, the Yukon native of the past lived in a world in which he constantly confronted various ramifications of superhuman power. . . . Much of his energy went into learning to cope with the fact" (1975:575). Every animal (indeed any object) was considered to have a spirit power or spiritual power associated with it; it was the "directing force" in the animal, allowing it to be killed and returning in another animal so long as it was respected (McClellan 1975:69, 91). Respect was crucial, for the spirit powers in many phenomena were "potentially harmful and quick to take offense if humans fail to accord them proper respect" (1975:69).

There were a large number of taboos associated with various animals, and violation of taboos associated with particular species could cause specific misfortunes. For example, a moose skull was to be kept out of the reach of dogs and a bone sliver was not to be used to extract marrow or no more moose would be killed; breaking taboos associated with mountain goats and sheep would cause snow and ice slides; if a wolverine was not respected, then the trapper's camp might burn down; clubbing a porcupine with an axe handle would produce a scarcity of porcupines (McClellan 1975:116–57 passim).

Bear, lynx, otter, and wolverine ranked above other species in their potential for harm. Mink also was powerful. Marten, beaver, muskrat, porcupine, rabbit, fox, and groundhog had the least potential for harm. (McClellan 1975:117–75 passim). McClellan notes that people "must always step warily with the more powerful members of the animal world, maintaining a respect relationship which is rather well defined" (1975:325).

Just how often disrespect—the violation of a taboo—caused illness or death is uncertain. Bears were a "powerful spiritual and genuine physical threat to humans" (McClellan 1975:125). Some taboos were linked to specific disorders: not to skin a lynx before bedtime could cause miscarriage; land otters might possess women and make them die; putting a finger in a mouse hole might cause warts; teasing a person with frogs could cause temporary insanity; and a boy who tied the legs of a frog together got sick (McClellan 1975:132, 143, 179, 543).

It is clear that the Southern Tutchone, Tagish, and Inland Tlingit believed that misfortune was also caused by shamans or witches. Shamans were assisted by a variety of spirit helpers and gave public performances in order to find game, cure sick people, foretell the future, or contact evil shamans or witches. If one person experienced bad luck, then he might have broken a taboo, been contaminated by a menstruating woman, or been the victim of witchcraft. If more than one person was affected, then it seems that witches were likely to be held responsible (McClellan 1975:530–66). McClellan notes that "much sickness was thought to be due to the machinations of other shamans and witches who could inject disease objects or bring about soul loss" (1975:542–43). Witches aimed to kill others; shamans attempted to suck out or blow away the sickness sent by a witch and send it back to the witch.

Epidemics and Sorcery

There is a noticeable lack of evidence to support the extension of Calvin Martin's hypothesis to the Kutchin or to other Athapaskan hunter-fishers. The Kutchin, who participated with great enthusiasm in the fur trade, did so not because of the removal of hypothetical constraints on overkill, but because they desired beads, dentalia shells, guns, and several other trade items. Although in many respects the Kutchin resembled their Northern Athapaskan neighbors to the southeast, they were different in that they distinguished among themselves on the basis of wealth. This at least was true of the mid-nineteenth-century Kutchin, those who had been involved in a trade for two generations, for whom beads were wealth and among whom shamans (who were paid for their ever-increasing services in this disease- and sorcerer-filled environment) were most affluent. Although there is a gap of thirty years in the ethnohistorical records between Alexander Mackenzie's first contact of the Kutchin and the preservation of post documents, there is no evidence either for epidemics, for the undermining of a religious system, or for apostatization during this early historic period. But there *is* evidence for acquisitive feelings and actions designed to satiate them.

Although the Kutchin believed that sickness and death could be caused by several factors, including taboo violation,[3] ethnohistorical evidence indicates that they tended to blame sorcerers for their epidemics. Other Northern Athapaskans also ascribed sickness to a variety of causes, although they tended to blame sorcerers for epidemics.

But the relationship between humans and animals was important. Northern Athapaskans respected animals, and believed that a violation of this respect could cause misfortune, including sickness. Violation of taboos associated with *particular* animal species might cause *specific* ailments. But at the same time, many, if not all, major sicknesses and epidemics could be traced to sorcerers. An outstanding example here are the Koyukon, who believed that taboo violation was punished by game scarcity and specific ailments, depending on the animal, but among whom (following Jetté, not Sullivan and Martin) there could be neither aboriginal nor postcontact "waste." Sorcerers were believed to cause illness, and at least two epidemics were blamed on Russians.

Data for the Chipewyan leaves several problems in interpretation. For one thing, not all Chipewyan bands reacted in the same way to the fur trade; some were attracted to it and became aggressive traders, while others remained in their traditional caribou-filled, beaver-scarce taiga habitat. Evidence for "despiritualization" at the time of Hearne's voyage (Martin 1978:145) is fuzzy: to what preceding time period, to what people or ethnographic observations, was Hearne comparing the Chipewyan?

In *Keepers of the Game*, Martin mentions the Chipewyan slaughter of caribou on several occasions (based on Hearne's observations)—they were "wasting game with gusto"—and regards a "never spare" legend as a type of postcontact rationalization (pp. 69–70, 109, 165). As alternate hypotheses, one might suggest (*a*) that so many caribou were killed mainly in August and September for the estimated twenty skins used by each Chipewyan each year (Hearne 1958:32, 127–28); (*b*) that the treatment of caribou by Matonabbee's group—devoted to the trade and following an acculturated leader of mixed heritage and with substantial exposure to the Euro-Canadians—was atypical (Hearne 1958:48, 220ff.); (*c*) that the kill was related to the trade in skins (Hearne 1958:115); or (*d*) that the kill was for nutritional purposes, since fat, potassium- and sodium-laden tongues, and marrow were sometimes the only parts taken (Hearne 1958:75).

Most important, perhaps, it may be ethnocentric to focus on any single portion of the animal as wasted: if skins were required but meat cannot be carried (or perhaps is not needed), or if tongues and marrow, but not the rest of the animal, are a nutritional requirement, then should the action of discarding the not-needed portion of the animal be labeled waste?

What is not a matter of dispute is that the Chipewyan blamed sorcerers for disease—and since sorcerers were often Eskimos, this occasioned revenge raids. In Hearne's time, leading Indians who died were "conjured to death"; "jugglers . . . threaten a secret revenge on any person, [and] it often proves fatal to that person" (Hearne 1958:143, 216–17).

Sorcerers were either other Athapaskans, Cree, Inuit, or Euro-Canadians. By the early nineteenth century, if not before, whites were regarded as powerful sorcerers (Back 1836:194). By the same time, Chipewyan correctly identified other humans, especially whites, as disease carriers. In the nineteenth century, Great Bear Lake Indians referred to whites as "those who bring death after them" (Petitot, in Morris 1972–73, 2:68). Twentieth-century Northern Athapaskans consistently have blamed whites for diseases: Chipewyan say that there was "no sickness business" in the past (Smith 1973:12), Kaska blame whites for colds and tuberculosis (Honigmann 1947:234), Han say that there was little sickness before whites arrived (Schmitter 1910:5; cf. Osgood 1971:58), Great Bear Lake Indians, that "Indians were never sick" before whites came (Osgood 1931:88), and the Southern Tutchone, that "nobody got sick long ago!" (McClellan 1975:223). In short, the idea "that sickness did not exist aboriginally" was very common (Osgood 1971:58; cf. McClellan 1975:223), and the coming of epidemics was linked to the arrival of Euro-Canadians.

There are a number of reasons why Chipewyan, in common with Kutchin and other Northern Athapaskans, would regard Euro-Canadians as shamans. One of the most important was probably Euro-Canadian immunity to diseases. In addition, Euro-Canadians did nothing to dissuade Indians from thinking that whites were medicine men. By the 1840s, "white people are said to be exempt from such dangers [of 'bad medicine'], their 'medicine' being the most powerful" (Richardson 1851, 2:22). One decade earlier, Indians regarded whites as "great medicine men" (Back 1833:194). In the early 1820s, the Yellowknives were amazed that Franklin knew beforehand of an eclipse, and Franklin said that he took advantage of this and told these Athapaskans about the Christian God (Franklin 1823:228). The Yellowknives called Franklin's companion, Dr. Richardson, the "Medicine Chief" and reported that "formerly numbers had died every year, but not a life had been lost since our [Franklin and Richardson's] arrival" (Franklin 1823:312). The foundations for this belief had been laid earlier, when, in the late eighteenth century, Samuel Hearne reported:

> Matonabbee, (who always thought me possessed of this art ["juggling"]), on his arrival at Prince of Wales's Fort in the Winter of 1778, informed me, that a man whom I had never seen but once, had treated him in such a manner that he was afraid of his life; in consequence of which he pressed me very much to kill him, though I was then several hundreds of miles distant: On which, to please this great man to whom I owed so much, and not expecting that any harm could possibly arise from it, I drew a rough sketch of two human figures on a piece of paper, in the attitude of wrestling: in the hand of one of them, I drew the figure of a bayonet pointing to the breast of the other. This is me, said I to Matonabbee, pointing to the figure which was holding the bayonet; and the other, is your enemy. Opposite to those figures I drew a pine-tree over which I placed a large human eye, and out of the tree projected a human hand. This paper I gave to Matonabbee, with instructions to make it as publicly known as possible. Sure enough, the following year, when he came in to trade, he informed me that the man was dead, though at that time he was not less than three hundred miles from Prince of Wales's Fort. He assured me that the man was in perfect health when he heard of my design against him; but almost immediately afterwards became quite gloomy, and refusing all kind of sustenance, in a very few days

died. After this I was frequently applied to on the same account, both by Matonabbee and other leading Indians, but never thought proper to comply with their requests; by which means I not only preserved the credit I gained on the first attempt, but always kept them in awe, and in some degree of respect and obedience to me. In fact, strange as it may appear, it is almost absolutely necessary that the chiefs at this place should profess something a little supernatural, to be able to deal with those people. [Hearne 1958:143]

Conclusion

In conclusion, Martin's hypothesis does not begin to explain the participation of the Kutchin and other Northern Athapaskans in the fur trade, nor does it account for why they trapped some fur bearers so vigorously as to cause local extinctions. While the Kutchin (and other Northern Athapaskans) were battered by diseases, which in some years were epidemic in duration and intensity, they attributed these diseases not to a hypothetical animal keeper, but to one of a number of causes in a complex system of etiology. In fact, the very complexity of etiology and the difficulties involved in reconstructing past ideology would seem to dictate extreme care with sources. However, in his treatment of the Koyukon, Martin has thrown care to the wind, by citing a cleric whose knowledge of the Koyukon was recent, brief, and superficial, compared with the ethnographic knowledge and reports of others. Furthermore, the ethnohistoric record bearing on the Koyukon, the Kutchin, and other Northern Athapaskans almost exclusively incriminates sorcery, not other factors, as held responsible for deaths from epidemic diseases. And, finally, from the earliest times of their involvement in the trade, the Kutchin and others demonstrated materialist and mercantilist tendencies, and these, it would seem, are sufficient to account for their exchange of pelts.

Notes

I wish to thank Annette McFadyen Clark, Richard Slobodin, and James VanStone for their helpful comments and suggestions on an earlier version of this paper; the Hudson's Bay Company for permission to examine and use their archives; and the American Philosophical Society for their support of archival research.

1. Following the ecozone classification made by McClellan 1970.
2. Honigmann 1970:230 suggests that the Kaska belief that witches can cause sickness diffused from the Tlingit via the Tahltan, for the Tlingit ascribe wasting, consumptive disease to witchcraft. I propose as an alternative hypothesis that the Kaska belief is more closely linked with an Athapaskan-wide pattern discussed in this paper.
3. Richard Slobodin (personal communication 27 September 1979) lists as folk explanations of disease and death, in addition to sorcery: taboo violation, supernatural malevolence, "curses" in certain families, and Christian-derived notion of divine punishment.

References Cited

Anderson, James
1849–59 Correspondence and Reports. MG 19 A 29 Public Archives of Canada, Ottawa.

Anonymous
1822 Notice of Attempts to Reach the Sea by Mackenzie's River since the Expedition of Sir Alexander Mackenzie. Wernerian Natural History Society, Edinburgh, Memoirs, 4:19–23.

Back, George
1836 Narrative of the Arctic Land Expedition to the Mouth of the Great Fish River, and Along the Shores of the Arctic Ocean, in the Years 1833, 1834, and 1835. London: John Murray.

Birket-Smith, Kaj
1930 Contributions to Chipewyan Ethnology. Report of the Fifth Thule Expedition, 1921–24, 6(3):1–113. Copenhagen.

Bishop, Charles A., and Arthur J. Ray
1976 Ethnohistoric Research in the Central Subarctic: Some Conceptual and Methodological Problems. Western Canadian Journal of Anthropology 6(1):116–44.

Cantwell, J. C.
1902 Report of the Operations of the U.S. Revenue Steamer Nunivak on the Yukon River Station, Alaska, 1899–1901. Washington, D.C.: Government Printing Office.

Clark, Annette M.
1970 Koyukon Athabascan Ceremonialism. Western Canadian Journal of Anthropology 2(2):80–88.

1974 Koyukuk River Culture. National Museum of Man

Mercury Series. Canadian Ethnology Service Paper
No. 18. Ottawa: National Museums of Canada.

Cooke, Allan, and Clive Holland

1971   Chronological List of Expeditions and Historical
Events in Northern Canada. The Polar Record
15(99):893–920.

Dall, William H.

1870   Alaska and Its Resources. Boston: Lee & Shepard.

Franklin, John

1823   Narrative of a Journey to the Shores of the Polar
Sea, in the Years 1819, 20, 21, and 22. London: John
Murray.

1828   Narrative of a Second Expedition to the Shores of
the Polar Sea, in the Years 1825, 1826, and 1827.
Philadelphia: Carey, Lea, and Carey.

Gillespie, Beryl C.

1975*a*   An Ethnohistory of the Yellowknives: A Northern
Athapaskan Tribe. *In* Contributions to Canadian
Ethnology, 1975, ed. D. B. Carlisle, pp. 191–245.
National Museum of Man Mercury Series. Cana-
dian Ethnology Service Paper No. 31. Ottawa:
National Museums of Canada.

1975*b*   Territorial Expansion of the Chipewyan in the Eighteenth Century. *In* Northern Athapaskan Conference, 1971, ed. Annette M. Clark, 2:350–88. National Museum of Man Mercury Series. Canadian
Ethnology Service Paper No. 27. Ottawa: National
Museums of Canada.

1976   Changes in Territory and Technology of the
Chipewyan. Arctic Anthropology 13(1):6–11.

Hardisty, William L.

1872   The Loucheux Indians. Annual Report of the
Smithsonian Institution for 1866, pp. 311–20.
Washington, D.C.

Hearne, Samuel

1958   A Journey from Prince of Wales Port in Hudson's

Bay to the Northern Ocean . . . in the Years 1769, 1770, 1771, and 1772. Richard Glover, ed. Toronto: Macmillan.

Honigmann, John J.

1946   Ethnography and Acculturation of the Fort Nelson Slave. Yale University Publications in Anthropology, No. 33. New Haven.

1947   Witch-Fear in Post-Contact Kaska Society. American Anthropologist 49:222–43.

1970   Witchcraft among Kaska Indians. *In* Systems of North American Witchcraft and Sorcery, ed. Deward E. Walker, pp. 221–38. Moscow, Idaho: University of Idaho.

Hudson's Bay Company Archives (HBCA), Winnipeg, Manitoba, Canada.

HBCA B.80a/1–19: Fort Good Hope Post Journals, 1822–1843.

HBCA B.157a/1–3: Peel River Post Journals, 1840–1844.

HBCA B.181a/1–14: Fort Resolution Post Journals, 1818–1840.

Isbister, A. K.

1845   Some Account of Peel River, N. America. Journal of the Royal Geographical Society of London 15 (part 2):332–45.

Janes, Robert R.

1975   The Athapaskan and the Fur Trade: Observations from Archaeology and Ethnohistory. Western Canadian Journal of Anthropology 5(3–4):159–86.

Jenness, Diamond, ed.

1956   The Chipewyan Indians: An Account by an Early Explorer. Anthropologica 3:15–33.

Jetté, Julius

1907   On the Medicine-Men of the Ten'a. Journal of the Royal Anthropological Institute of Great Britain and Ireland 37:157–86.

1911   On the Supersititions of the Ten'a Indians (Middle
       Part the Yukon Valley, Alaska). Anthropos 6:95–
       108, 241–59, 602–15, 699–723.
Jones, Strachan
1872   The Kutchin Tribes. Annual Report of the Smithso-
       nian Institution for 1866, pp. 320–27. Washington,
       D.C.
Keith, George
1889–90 Letters to Mr. Roderick McKenzie. *In* Les Bourgeois
       de la Compagnie du Nord-Quest, ed. L. R. Mas-
       son, 2:65–127. Quebec: A Cote.
Kennicott, Robert
1869   The Journal of Robert Kennicott, May 19, 1859–
       February 11, 1862. Transactions of the Chicago
       Academy of Sciences 1 (part 2):132–226. Chicago.
Kir(k)by, William West
1872   A Journey to the Youcan Russian America. Annual
       Report of the Smithsonian Institution for 1866, pp.
       416–20. Washington, D.C.
Krech, Shepard III
1976   The Eastern Kutchin and the Fur Trade, 1800–1860.
       Ethnohistory 23:213–35.
1978   On the Aboriginal Population of the Kutchin. Arctic
       Anthropology 15(1):89–103.
1979*a* The Nakotcho Kutchin: A Tenth Aboriginal Kutchin
       Band? Journal of Anthropological Research 35:
       109–21.
1979*b* Interethnic Relations in the Lower Mackenzie River
       Region. Arctic Anthropology 16(2):102–22.
1980   Introduction: "Reconsiderations" and Ethnohistori-
       cal Research. Arctic Anthropology 17(2):in press.
McClellan, Catharine
1970   Introduction to Special Issue: Athabascan Studies.
       Western Canadian Journal of Anthropology 2(1):
       vi–xix.
1975   My Old People Say: An Ethnographic Survey of

Southern Yukon Territory. National Museum of Man Publications in Ethnology No. 6. Ottawa: National Museums of Canada.

McKennan, Robert A.
1965   The Chandalar Kutchin. Arctic Institute of North America Technical Paper No. 17. Montreal.

McKenzie, Alexander
1805–6   Journal of Great Bear Lake. Archives of British Columbia, Victoria.

Mackenzie, Alexander
1970   The Journals and Letters of Sir Alexander Mackenzie. W. Kaye Lamb, ed. London: Cambridge University Press.

MacNeish, June Helm
1954   Contemporary Folk Beliefs of a Slave Indian Band. Journal of American Folklore 67:185–98.

Martin, Calvin
1978   Keepers of the Game: Indian-Animal Relationships and the Fur Trade. Berkeley: University of California Press

Mason, J. Alden
1946   Notes on the Indians of the Great Slave Lake Area. Yale University Publications in Anthropology, No. 34. New Haven.

Michael, Henry N.
1967   Lieutenant Zagoskin's Travels in Russian America, 1842–1844. Arctic Institute of North American Anthropology of the North: Translations from Russian Sources, No. 7. Toronto: University of Toronto Press.

Morris, Margaret W.
1972–73 Great Bear Lake Indians: A Historical Demography and Human Ecology. Parts 1 and 2. The Musk-Ox 11:3–27, 12:58–80.

Murray, Alexander Hunter
1910   Journal of the Yukon, 1847–48. Publications of the

Canadian Archives, No. 4. Ottawa.

Osgood, Cornelius

1931 The Ethnography of the Great Bear Lake Indians. Canada Department of Mines, Annual Report for 1931, Bulletin X10. 70:31–93.

1936 Contributions to the Ethnography of the Kutchin. Yale University Publications in Anthropology, No. 14. New Haven.

1971 The Han Indians: A Compilation of Ethnographic and Historical Data on the Alaska-Yukon Boundary Area. Yale University Publications in Anthropology, No. 74. New Haven.

Parker, James

1972 The Fur Trade and Chipewyan Indian. Western Canadian Journal of Anthropology 3(1):43–57.

Peers, Augustus R.

1847–53 Journal of (Daily) Occurrences (Peel's River Papers) MG 19 D12. Public Archives of Canada, Ottawa.

Rich, E. E., ed.

1938 Journal of Occurrences in the Athabasca Department by George Simpson, 1820 and 1821, and Report. Toronto: The Champlain Society.

Richardson, John

1851 Arctic Searching Expedition: A Journal of a Boat Voyage through Rupert's Land and the Arctic Sea, in Search of the Discovery Ships under Command of Sir John Franklin. 2 vols. London: Longman, Brown, Green and Longmans.

Ross, Bernard

1858 Letter from Mr. Ross to George Gibbs, with detailed information relative to Chipewyan tribes, with abstract of MacKenzie River Dist., June 1, 1858. MS 144A, Bureau of American Ethnology, National Anthropology Archives, Smithsonian Institution.

Schmitter, Ferdinand

1910 Upper Yukon Native Customs and Folk-Lore. Smithsonian Miscellaneous Collections 56(4):1–30.

Sharp, Henry S.
1977   The Chipewyan Hunting Unit. American Ethnologist 4(2):377–93.

Simpson, Thomas
1843   Narrative of the Discoveries on the North Coast of America. London: Richard Bentley.

Smith, David Merrill
1973   Inkonze: Magico—Religious Beliefs of Contact—Traditional Chipewyan Trading at Fort Resolution, N.W.T., Canada. National Museum of Man Mercury Series. Canadian Ethnology Service Paper No. 6. Ottawa: National Museums of Canada.

Smith, James G. E.
1975   The Ecological Basis of Chipewyan Socio-Territorial Organization. In Northern Athapaskan Conference, 1971, ed. Annette M. Clark, 2:389–461. National Museum of Man Mercury Series. Canadian Ethnology Service Paper No. 27. Ottawa: National Museums of Canada.

1976   Local Band Organization of the Caribou Eater Chipewyan in the Eighteenth and Early Nineteenth Centuries. Western Canadian Journal of Anthropology 6(1):72–90.

1978   Economic Uncertainty in an "Original Affluent Society": Caribou and Caribou Eater Chipewyan Adaptive Strategies. Arctic Anthropology 15(1): 68–88.

Smith, James G. E., and Ernest S. Burch
1979   Chipewyan and Inuit in the Central Canadian Subarctic, 1613–1977. Arctic Anthropology 16(2):76–101.

Sullivan, Robert J.
1942   The Ten'a Food Quest. Anthropological Series, Vol. 11. Washington, D.C.: The Catholic University of America Press.

Wentzel, Willard F.
1805–6 Fragment of Journal by Wentzel at Grand River near

McKenzie River, 1805 and 1806. MG 19 E/1, Selkirk, pp. 9298–9308. Public Archives of Canada, Ottawa.

1889–90 Letters to the Hon. Roderick McKenzie. *In* Les Bourgeois de la Compagnie du Nord-Quest, ed. L. F. Masson, 1:67–153. Quebec: A Cote.

CHAPTER SIX

THE NATURE OF
EVIL: OF WHALES
AND SEA OTTERS

LYDIA T. BLACK

IN THIS PAPER I examine in the light of the Aleut data the basic thesis proposed by Calvin Martin that throughout the American Subarctic, and possibly throughout the continent, Indians under European onslaught redefined their relationship to animals, heretofore conceptualized as benevolent partners of more or less equal status within a unitary, harmonious order, and that Indians then declared war on animals, blaming them for an assortment of evils, with a resultant indiscriminate slaughter and depletion of various species.

I find this thesis inapplicable to the Aleut situation, and I find the assumptions, explicit and implicit, on which the thesis rests fallacious in the light of anthropological theory and the ethnographic record.

In the following sections, I briefly outline the bases for my objections to several assumptions of the general order, then turn to a sketch of Aleut environment, precontact subsistence, the structure of the fur trade in Russian Alaska, Aleut attitudes to and the history of the commercially exploited species, and, finally, to the conversion to Christianity of the Aleuts in the eighteenth century. I conclude by demonstrating that in the Aleut area, conversion to Christianity preceded by better than a century the critical depletion of commercially hunted animals and that changes in Aleut hunting practices are directly attributable to changes in the economic structure, to new economic pressures, and to the introduction of firearms. I suggest that a causal relation between conversion to Christianity—that is, the change in Aleut belief system—and changes in the economics of the chase cannot be demonstrated.

General Considerations and Points of Theory

Calvin Martin affirms the changes in ideology, specifically a change in the conceptualization of the human-animal relationship, and not the desire for European goods and trade, caused massive overhunting of various fur-bearers by Indians. Martin maintains that the Indians, faced with new, often epidemic, diseases that were brought to the American continent by Europeans and that reached the Indians prior to any actual contact, interpreted this novel and stressful situation in the light of pre-existing ideology and concluded that the animals had turned against the humans, causing death through widespread disease. In response, the Indians "declared war" on the animals in an effort to exterminate these creatures, now seen as inimical to the human race.

In a sense, Martin posits the centrality of ideology in structuring human behavior. This stance is not new and is widely discussed in the philosophy and theology of our times, foremost by Ortega y Gasset (1961). The notion has also been discussed in anthropological theory (Coulanges 1956; Durkheim 1965; Redfield 1953), most recently by Geertz (1956). It is recognized that ideological change is inseparable from cultural change and that ideologies, like cultures, are best analyzed as a process. Moreover, it has been long established in anthropological theory that ideological changes are most radical and observable in times of stress. Thus, Martin's general thesis—that there was a transformation in Indian thinking under the impact of the social dislocation and concommitant psychological stress which occurred as a result of European conquest—is valid enough. What is at issue is the cause-effect relationship between various subsystems of a culture in the process of change and the nature of the ideological transformation in particular cases. Martin's insistence on one-way causality, and his specific thesis that the transformation in Indian thinking meant that animals became conceptualized as disease- and death-causing agents, is open to question. His insistence on the essential differentness of the Indian can be challenged on philosophical grounds (Mannheim 1936; Powdermaker 1966) and out of anthropological research experience (Chandler 1974). Martin claims that this essential differentness of the Indian—the Indianness (Chandler 1974)— rested on the concept of a life-giving power inherent in the universe, extraneous but accessible to humans through ritual action. But this concept may, in fact, be characterized as virtually universal. Moreover, the view of the human-animal relationship as special, characterized by the notion of Master(s) of Animals, which Martin, also claims to be unique to the Indian, has an extremely wide distribution. Occurrence of such notions is thoroughly documented for Eurasia and is found in Africa.[1]

Martin's notion that Indians embarked upon a campaign of extermination once they had decided that the animals had become the enemies of humans requires that death be conceptualized as annihilation. With the exception of certain segments of modern Western-educated strata, men universally conceptualize death as transformation. In fact, death—or more often, certain types of death—is conceptualized as a determinant of the fate and destination of the deceased's essential being. Metamorphosis is a special kind of such transformation (Black 1973).

The ethnographic record is against extension of Martin's thesis to all groups on the American continent; the various aboriginal groups adhered to different belief systems, and their conceptualization of causality and of death varied. The conceptualization of all Europeans as a single undifferentiated whole labeled "the whites" cannot be sustained, and neither can the notion that these whites adhered to a single monolithic belief system labeled "Christianity." The Europeans varied among themselves even more than the Indians, and it follows that contact situations were structured differently in various areas.

The projection of a single model of conversion process predicated on the notion that all conversion is a result of organized missionary activity is not valid. Also invalid is the projection of the model of the fur trade, derived from the eastern Subarctic experience, to areas where fur trade was structured differently and where species other than beaver were hunted. In the Aleutian area the two species valued symbolically, whales and sea otters, were depleted at the end of the nineteenth century and then, not by natives but by Euro-American whalers and commercial sea otter hunters.

The Aleuts

The group we know as Aleuts is a creation of postcontact times. Prior to contact, the inhabitants of the Aleutian Archipelago, from Port Moller on the Alaska Peninsula in the east to Attu Island in the west, formed many political units and at least two, possibly three, culturally and linguistically distinct populations.[2]

Aleuts were settled through an island chain of more than 100 islands extending a linear distance of nearly 1,250 miles (Laughlin and Aigner 1975; cf. McCartney 1975:288). The population was sparse, and there was reportedly a tradition of a constant diminution, ascribed in the Aleut folklore to intensive intergroup warfare, changes in availability of major animal species, and periodic lack of subsistence resources (Veniaminov 1840; Bergsland 1979, 1959).[3]

The first Europeans to penetrate the area were Russians in 1741. Hitherto the Aleuts had lived in relative isolation. They were, of course, in contact with their Eskimo and Indian neighbors on the American continent. There is also evidence of infrequent, sporadic contact with Asiatics, specifically, some Siberian native groups, the Kuriles (Ainu), and the Japanese (Khlebnikov 1979; Wheaton 1945).

Smallpox did not reach the Aleutians until 1838, and then only the eastern Aleutians. The spread of this disease was checked by sheer distance, lack of regular communication between settlements, and the introduction of vaccination (RAC; Khlebnikov 1979; Netsvetov 1980; Veniaminov 1840; Blaschke 1848). In the eighteenth century the Russians observed two epidemic diseases which presumably had also occurred in precontact times; at any rate, the Russians reported these diseases as being unfamiliar to them. The symptoms of one are indicative of the pulmonary form of Sylvatic plague, while the descriptions of the other are somewhat reminiscent of tularemia. Occurrences of certain epidemic diseases can be documented for distinct geographic segments of the Aleutian archipelago.[4]

For subsistence, the aboriginal population in precontact times relied exclusively on marine fauna. The islands are of tectonic and volcanic origin and have no terrestrial animals, with the exception of Unimak in the east. Elsewhere, foxes, rats, mice, and ground squirrels are a very recent introduction, mostly by human agency (see below). All available forms of marine fauna were used as food and a source of technological materials. The most desirable species—sea otter, fur seal, seal (hair or harbor predominantly), and sea lion—were hunted primarily in the open sea. These animals have an uneven distribution, and not all were available in all localities. Moreover, most of the species, and especially the fur seal, were available only seasonally or hunted seasonally (sea otter). Whales were a major resource, but only beached carcasses were utilized throughout the Aleut area, and only the Eastern Aleuts hunted whales in very limited numbers.

All marine mammal species hunted in precontact times continued to be taken in postcontact times for subsistence, and two of the species, the sea otter and the fur seal, for trade. Eventually, after 1799, these two fur-bearers became a commercial crop and were hunted for pelts, though the flesh continued to provide a major source of food. Aboriginal hunting technology and practices were maintained, with the main difference being in the disposition of pelts: whereas in precontact times Aleuts dressed their womenfolk in skins of sea otter and fur seal, in postcontact times they delivered the pelts to the Russian American Company.

The Aleut belief system is poorly known and at this time is difficult to reconstruct. The opportunity was lost a century ago when investigators assumed that the old beliefs and knowledge were lost because the Aleuts professed themselves devout Christians and, to a large extent, had abandoned the external symbols of the aboriginal belief system—or so it was believed. Nevertheless, some vestiges remain even today, although extreme caution must be exercised in interpreting recently obtained information. It is possible, to some extent, to infer Aleut concepts with regard to the animals they hunted on the basis of data in recorded folklore, scattered observations in reports by early observers, and ethnosemantics.[5] In general, marine mammals, with the exception of whales, were conceptualized as transformed humans. Apparently, their remains were disposed of in an orderly fashion, though on this point the information is extremely limited and the significance of various modes of disposal not clear (Merck 1937; Sarychev 1802:127).

Disease causation was conceptualized as an expression of the evil principle inherent in the universe that opposed the good, creative principle and power. This evil was seen as loosed upon a man or his community by transgression against the Aleut system of values and moral order. Once loosed, evil could manifest itself as spirits which could metamorphose into various shapes or infest a locality. Shamans divined the causes of disease and usually ascribed it to a sinful action committed by the patient or the patient's close kin through the instigation of an evil spirit (Sarychev 1802:142, 165). One could take preventive measures against evil influence, and Aleuts believed in individual spirit protectors, linked to individual human beings in various ways, including names and talismans. These protectors ensured success for the individual in hunt and war and prevented such misfortunes as illness, discord, or death through disease, which were ultimately caused, as mentioned above, by the nonpersonified evil. It seems, however, that the power of the protectors sometimes was not sufficient if the moral character of the hunter was at fault (see below).

Shamans, excluded at least among the Eastern Aleuts from playing any role in familial and seasonal rites (Veniaminov 1840), were present among all Aleut groups. Their function was to ward off evil and its works; to avert misfortunes, such as lack of food; to prevent ill luck; to prevent and cure illness; to foretell and change the weather; and to foretell future events. There is no evidence whatsoever that animals either were or could be conceptualized as disease-causing agents.

The European Fur Trade

It is convenient to consider the fur trade in the Aleutian area within a time perspective. Several major phases can be distinguished and within each of these, shorter, overlapping periods, each characterized by diverse structure of financing, labor units, marketing, and technology and by different patterns of Aleut participation. A rough time table, derived mainly from data in Makarova (1968), Tikhmenev (1978), Khlebnikov (1979), and the records of the Russian American Company, is presented below. It should be noted that no sharp temporal boundary may be drawn between the suggested periods, and the chronology is intended solely as a guide to understanding the changes in the structure of the Aleutian fur trade.

1745–1770. This is a time of unrestricted enterprise, organized by and large locally in eastern Siberia and financed by shares. Shareholders participate in actual voyages. The crew are shareholders also. Large numbers of eastern Siberians, predominantly Kamchadal, are among the crew. The interaction with the Aleuts is characterized by sporadic and localized conflict, intermittent barter, and the establishment of alliances between individual skippers and/or foremen and individual local chiefs or notables. Some technological innovation occurs, notably introduction of the Kamchadal method of taking sea otters by net and fox trapping. Toward the end of the period, Aleut hunting on order, for barter, increases.

End of the 1770s to end of the 1780s. Large capital, not controlled locally, enters into the trade. Competition between individual entrepreneurs or companies is on the increase. There are larger ships and larger crews, with a smaller proportion of Siberian natives among the crews, but more Siberian tribes represented. Fewer shares are in the hands of actual participants in the voyages, and proportionally more shares in the hands of the absentee financiers. There is more pressure to show fast and larger profits, pressure for larger catches to provide capital for expansion. As a consequence of this pressure and intercompany competition, skippers compete for Aleut alliances. Individual skippers, out for a quick profit, rely less on Aleut alliances and more on direct force to ensure Aleut "cooperation." The Aleuts are more and more drawn into the fur trade both through intensification of barter and direct engagement in the labor force, both voluntary and through impressment. Reliance on Aleut hunters increases.

1786–1799. Economic power is consolidated in the hands of a very few merchants. There are initial efforts to establish a fur trading monopoly, and accelerated competition for virtual (but not yet legal) monopoly. In this competition, the Aleuts are squeezed economically, as skippers, themselves under increased pressures, even rob Aleut villages of food stores. It is during this period that reports of overhunting or potential overhunting of various hauling and breeding grounds are voiced. Charges of "mismanagement" are made by various competitors. There is no doubt that resource management—that is, preservation of fur-bearers for future exploitation—figures in the arguments advanced by the proponents of the monopoly. The early Russian merchant-hunters understand the habits of their prey very well, and fear of overhunting a particular hunting ground is a motivating force in eastward expansion: the skippers do not like to be "crowded." It is not possible at this point to reconstruct actual animal populations and population fluctuations for this period. Until there is a thorough statistical analysis of the reported catches, with attention paid to the extent of the geographic area hunted and the exact times in which particular catches were obtained, no statement can be made of how heavily overhunted, if at all, the Aleutians were.

1799–1817. The crown grants monopoly rights in 1799 to the company organized by Grigorii Shelikhov. This company eventually becomes the Russian American Company, with virtually absolute power in Russian America, both economic and governmental. The crown, officially and in writing, informs Aleut leaders of the new order of things. On the ground, the Aleuts lose out, as they can no longer maneuver and manipulate rival merchants. The control exercised by the Russian American Company is uneven throughout the area; this control is extended only gradually, over time, from the center on Kodiak to the Alaskan mainland and southeast into Tlingit territory. In the Aleutian region, the Alaskan Peninsula and the Shumagin Islands are the first areas brought under company control, then the Eastern Aleutians with the center at Unalaska, and the Pribilof Islands. The Western Aleutians, from Amukhta Pass on, formally incorporated into company territory, remain controlled from Okhotsk. Communication is sporadic (about once every five years), personnel scant and in some areas nonexistent. Gradually, the Aleut communities here revert to subsistence hunting. Some islands in the Andreanofs and the Rat Islands serve as refuge for Eastern Aleuts escaping from the Russian American Company's control. During this period, known as the

Baranov years, the profit motive is paramount, and the exploitation of the population under the company's effective control is at its peak, in direct violation of the terms of the monopoly charter and various government edicts specifying fair and equitable treatment of Alaskan aboriginal peoples. Only occasionally does the company's management look over its metaphorical shoulder in order not to offend the crown too blatantly. In the Eastern Aleutians, the majority of the Aleuts are impressed into the labor force, though independent Aleut communities tied to the company through systematic trade continue to exist. In the Western Aleutians, such communities survive until a much later time, even into the American period. This is the period of the forced resettlement of groups of Eastern Aleuts to the previously uninhabited Pribilof Islands, to Sitka, and other areas of mainland Alaska.

1817–1867. This period sees the establishment and development of governmental control over the Russian American Company and may be characterized as the period of the rule of the law. High-ranking naval officers are appointed as governors, accountable not only to the company's head office but also to the government and responsible not only for profits but for the implementation of state policies in the colonies. With the passage of time, reasons of state increasingly outweigh immediate short-term considerations. Future development of the colonies is stressed as a goal, and an attempt is made to develop a population native to the American soil but with strong cultural ties to Russia—the creoles.[6] Social advancement is made possible and creoles and Aleuts occupy middle-managerial decisionmaking positions. Education and literacy in native and Russian languages are fostered. During this period conservation measures are introduced and enforced,[7] though the debate about the possible depletion of the hunting grounds never ceased. Catches of major fur-bearers are controlled by annual quotas, prohibition on killing female and young, and, in the case of sea otters, rotation of hunting grounds.

The Aleuts directly employed by the company are assigned salaries. Those who are not in the company's employ but participate in the fur-trade network are paid in accordance with an official schedule. The Aleuts constitute the major element in the labor force, and they continue to employ their own aboriginal hunting methods.

Thus, deliberate conservation measures, the structure of the hunting units, and the hunting methods all impose limits on the catch. For example, in the Western Aleutians—that is, from Seguam to the Commandor Islands—no more than 300 sea otters were taken annually (Bergsland 1979; RAC).

The depletion of the major fur-bearers—the fur seals and the otters—did not occur until after 1867. When sovereignty over Alaska passed from Russia to the United States, Alaska's fur wealth was still intact (Alaska Journal 1893).

1867–1911. In the American period, the taking of fur-bearers is organized basically on the principle of laissez-faire, with the exception of the fur seal breeding grounds in the Pribilofs, where a government controlled monopoly is responsible for fur seal taking. Elsewhere, pelagic sealing and sea otter hunting becomes the order of the day, so that both the Pribilof fur seal herd and sea otters become endangered.[8] The diminution of the Pribilof fur seal herd in the early 1880s moves the U.S. government to action, which eventually leads to the treaty of 1892 between the United States and Great Britain to submit the question of U.S. jurisdiction in the Bering Sea to international arbitration (see Bering Sea Tribunal 1895). The United States identifies the main cause of the diminution of the fur seal herd as pelagic sealing. Following arbitration, pelagic sealing regulation is instituted but proves unsatisfactory, so that in 1911 Great Britain, Canada, Japan, Russia, and the United States sign an international agreement prohibiting pelagic sealing altogether. During the American period, pelagic hunting is conducted directly by European, Canadian, U.S., and Japanese fur hunters and also by Aleuts employed by Euro-American owners of hunting vessels. While under Russian management, however, Aleut hunters had been prohibited from using firearms in hunting sea otter, and the ancient atlatl continued to be the chief weapon; in the American period the musket, and then the breech-loading rifle, become the chief instruments of taking the marine furbearers. The introduction of firearms as hunting weapons is one of the main causes of rapid diminution of the sea otter.

The demise of the sea otter in Alaskan waters in the decade of the 1880s–1890s is documented by Calvin L. Hooper, captain of the U.S. Revenue Cutter Service, in command of the Bering Sea Patrol. In his report to the secretary of the treasury, dated 1897, Hooper, on the basis of first-hand data, states that the depletion of sea otter grounds has occurred within the decade of his report and that it is due to pelagic hunting with the use of firearms, and to the establishment of canneries in the areas of sea otter concentration, which are polluting the environment and causing sea otters to abandon their hauling grounds. Hooper points out that the Aleuts derive their subsistence, and maintain their economic independence, through exploitation of sea otters, that the Aleuts are integrated into the economic network of the sea otter trade, and that uncontrolled hunting by outsiders would spell the end of the sea otter and the end of Aleut economic independence and even Aleut survival (1897:11). He urges the U.S. government to take this fact into account in promulgating regulations for preservation of the sea otter and control of the sea otter hunt. He wrote: "It is not only to preserve the [sea] otter, the most beautiful and valuable fur-bearing animal in the world, but to preserve it for the benefit of the natives who have been dependent upon it for more than a century, and who will be reduced to suffering and want without it" (1897:11). Hooper suggests that white hunters be excluded from the sea otter hunt, pointing out that the natives adhere to long-established conservation practices. He believes that not only the sea otter but a financially independent native people will survive if the whites are banned (pp. 9–14). Consequently, he incorporates into his suggestions for regulations governing the sea otter hunt the proposal that "no person shall be allowed to kill sea otters within the limits of Alaska territory, or the waters thereof, from or by use of any boat or vessel other than ordinary two-hatch skin covered bidarka or the open Yakutat canoe" (p. 15).

Hooper's recommendations either are not followed or are circumvented. Hunting from schooners or by baydarka fleets carried by schooners to distant hauling grounds, by Euro-Americans and by hired Aleuts, all armed with firearms, continues.

By 1911, sea otters have almost totally disappeared in Alaskan waters. In that year, a schooner hunting out of Unalaska takes only three sea otters during the season in an area extending from Unalaska to Kodiak. This schooner carries a party of Aleut hunters, the best in the area, but according to Henry Swanson, a participant in the hunt (interviewed in 1975), none of them used, and only one knew how to use the ancient dart-thrower, the atlatl, used exclusively during the Russian period and still in use as late as 1890 by Aleuts who hunted sea otter independently (Fassett 1890; see Appendix for the Aleut petition to President Cleveland). That very year, 1911, following the international agreements, all killings of sea otter becomes illegal.[9]

Foxes were flourishing as a commercial crop in the Aleutians, providing an excellent source of money both to Aleut and non-Aleut entrepreneurs, up to World War II. In the postwar years, under the pressure from ecologically minded but ill-informed groups, trapping of fox was prohibited in many regions or restricted (depending on the locality), with the result that the increased fox population demolished nests, eggs, and young of various protected species of birds, before the foxes starved. Recently, the Polar foxes on Attu had to be poisoned by Fish and Game personnel, as they were endangering the emperor geese there.

Whales, of course, did not constitute a commercial crop during the Russian period, though some (at most sixty, on the average about thirty, per year) were taken in the Eastern Aleutians by native hunters as a subsistence resource. The whale was the prey of the Euro-American whaler. In fact, the whale population was commercially exploited in the Aleutians until World War II and a major whaling company, controlled from Minneapolis, maintained a blubbering station on Akutan until that time (see, *inter alia*, Birkeland 1926; my field data, 1976).

The fur seal, the hair seal, and sea lions, always hunted by the Aleuts, still flourish. It remains to establish what the attitudes of the Aleuts were toward their prey.

Conceptualization of the Hunted Species

As is apparent from the preceding discussion, only two of the species important in Aleut economics prior to contact, the sea otter and the fur seal, became major commercial "crops." The third economically and symbolically significant animal, the whale, was not hunted commercially by Aleuts at any time, while the animals which constituted one of the major sources of commercial revenue until recent times, the arctic and the common fox, were not hunted in precontact times.

The common fox (*Vulpes fulva*), in variety (red, black, silver, and cross), was at the time of contact abundant only in the Eastern Aleutians and then not on all islands (Murie 1959). The Aleuts considered the flesh of the animal inedible, and the fur and body parts were not used, except possibly by shamans in some apotropaic rites, but the evidence on this last point is practically nil. In some folklore tales, recorded in the twentieth century (Iokhel'son, Ms.), an evildoer, a woman, is metamorphosed into a fox, but such folkloristic record is rare and may be a recent innovation.

Fox trapping was introduced by the Russians, who distributed fox traps to the Aleuts at first contact in the Eastern Aleutians (Andreyev 1948). In the Western Aleutians, the Russians introduced both the animal and the trap. The arctic (polar or blue) fox (*Alopex lagopus*) was introduced on Attu Island in 1750 by Andrean Tolstykh, who brought a breeding pair from Bering Island. The cropping of the readily multiplying animals began around 1756 (Andreyev 1948; Liapunova 1979).

Subsequently, both common and arctic foxes were "planted" on various islands, by species, so that each island served as an unfenced fur-animal farm: between 1823 and 1826, breeding pairs of blue foxes were transported to the Andreanof and Rat Islands from the Pribilofs, and silver and cross foxes from Sitka to Amlia and Adak, respectively (RAC). In 1843/44 black foxes were introduced on Amchitka. The foxes fed on intertidal fauna, birds, and occasional rodents. If they were not cropped, they endangered the bird population, a major resource of food and clothing materials, causing Aleuts to complain about the fox menace (West 1938; Bergsland 1959). In fact, ground squirrels were transported to various islands from the Alaskan Peninsula and Unimak Island in order to provide food for "planted" foxes or even for foxes where they occurred naturally (Murie 1959). Some trappers even hunted seal and left the carcasses for their foxes (Wheaton 1945).

It is my impression that the Aleuts, like the white fur trappers, considered these animals purely crop animals.

Fur seals in precontact times were hunted where available in the interisland straits during the seasonal migration of the herd to and from the breeding ground, the Pribilof Islands. The Aleuts knew of the Pribilof Islands in precontact times, but they were not inhabited and because of distance, not visited. The Russians discovered these islands in 1786, and from that time on, Aleuts were taken to the Pribilof Islands in Russian ships, first seasonally and later (1823–26) as permanent settlers. Here, the animals were killed on the hauling grounds by clubbing, the method developed on the Commandor Islands by the Russians since 1740s. The furs were taken by the Russians, the meat used as food by both the Aleuts and the Russians and often transported to supply villages with lesser resource bases.

Aleuts distinguished fur seals terminologically from other

seal species but conceptualized them, in common with all other seals, as transformed humans (Golder 1905, 1909a). Seals originated when bodies or parts of bodies (usually the head), of murder victims were thrown into the sea by murderers. There is some slight indication that in precontact times, when Aleuts took the fur seals at sea, or rather, in interisland channels, they preferred taking or restricted the taking to adult males—a practice later incorporated into conservation practices under Russian management.[10]

In general, if any inference is possible, the most likely hypothesis is that the Aleuts regarded seal-hunting as a contest between a man and a man transformed into an animal. One may surmise that ritual preparation for the hunt approximated that for combat, and in some instances that for death (as it did in the walrus hunt, to be specific; see Kashevarov-Yanovskiy correspondence 1862).

There is absolutely no evidence that the taking of animals increased because of a conceptual redefinition of the hunter-prey relationship. On the contrary, the increased fur seal kill by methods introduced by the Russians would be consonant with the Aleut ideal that a man proved himself in battle by killing as many enemies as he could, and as a hunter, by taking as many animals as he could.

Sea otters were conceptualized as transformed human beings. They were created by the benevolent deity to assuage the grief of parents who lost their children through sin: an incestuous brother-sister pair who committed suicide (or, in other versions, murder-suicide) by throwing themselves into the sea. Sea otters were believed to possess many human qualities and to function not at all as disease-causing agents but, on the contrary, as moral arbitrators of human behavior. They judged both individual and public morality; sea otters withdrew from an amoral person, just as Aleuts withdrew their social approval from a transgressor of social mores. A man who could not insure the fidelity of his wife, whose sister became unchaste, or one who was immoderate, lazy, slothful, etc., would be subjected to ridicule by the sea otters: they would cavort around the kayak, play and laugh, but remain tantalizingly out of his reach (Veniaminov 1840, 2:135, 154–56). In contrast to the whale hunter, a sea otter hunter was apparently not subjected to social isolation or an elaborate ritual of preparation through fast and abstinence, nor to any ritual of purification after a successful hunt: his success in the sea otter hunt was ensured by his own good character and moral probity, and, if he was lucky, by the possession of a talisman, a gift, especially cast ashore for him by the sea. This talisman, either male or female, served to attract sea otters of the opposite sex (Veniaminov 1840, 2:131–32, 134–36). The hunter adorned his person and his kayak in such a way as to appeal to sea otters' human qualities.

Three methods of sea otter taking were in use: by the surround (Scammon 1870; Fassett 1890; Alaska Journal 1893; Hooper 1897; Veniaminov 1840; Netsvetov 1980), by net (Netsvetov 1980; Alaska Journal 1893), and in the west, by hand (Netsvetov 1980). Of these three methods, two, the surround and by hand, were aboriginal, and both may be interpreted as contest or combat. The surround resembles the tactics of an Aleut sea battle (or the other way around). As the sea otter was driven to exhaustion and eventually drowned, or was clubbed when it could not dive anymore, so the enemy was surrounded, his kayak overturned, and he was not allowed to come up for air. Even stronger is the analogy in the most ancient of methods, only described, to my knowledge, by Netsvetov. Here the hunter entered the lair of the sea otter, a semisubmerged cave, in order to take the animal without weapons of any kind, knowing that he himself might be mauled or even killed by the enraged beast. Interestingly, the hunter brought with him, under his waterproof clothing, flint and tinder and a lamp which he tried first of all to light. It is believed that the sea otter, not being able to tolerate this light, would rush to extinguish the flame, and in this rush would give the hunter the opportunity to grab the animal near the tail—the source of motion control (my field data)—and then club it to death.

Archaeological evidence indicates that in precontact times the sea otter was the most hunted animal. However, the sea otter hunt, by the surround method employed by Aleuts until the 1890s, is a very labor-intensive enterprise. It demands the participation of from twelve to eighteen single- or double-hatched kayaks, engaging a minimum of twelve hunters. Sea otters are hunted only in summer, only in calm weather, preferably on a sunny day. Days may go by without a single animal being taken; seldom are two or three animals taken in one day. Since the Aleuts believed that close proximity of human habitation would cause the sea otters to abandon their hauling grounds, the travel to the hunting areas required several days. Moreover, there was a sort of rotation of visits to the hauling grounds, apparently in precontact as well as postcontact times. It seems that Aleut usages contributed significantly to the development of Russian conservation policies (see Hooper 1897). Until 1867 and the extensive killing of animals resting on shore (see Alaska Journal 1893), the herds were maintained in sufficient strength for a variety of effective reasons, not the least of which were the manpower requirements of the hunt.

The whale, though commercially exploited only by Euro-American whalers, was symbolically as important as the sea otter. There is no doubt that whales occupied a special position in the Aleut world view, especially among the Eastern Aleuts; but what this position was cannot be determined with certainty now.

Taking of a whale (or beaching of a whale carcass) was a joyous occasion for the community. The man whose dart was found imbedded in the whale's body enjoyed the right to divide the carcass. A great deal of social prestige accrued to him. Yet his fate was believed not to be an enviable one: if a whale hunter did not die young, he was expected to become hopelessly insane. Consequently, not every man became a whale hunter. A man, if he chose to become one, was set apart from society in a way we cannot determine at present.

Hunting whales was conceptualized as a solitary enterprise,

even if a number of whale hunters set out in pursuit of the same whale (Veniaminov 1840). The enterprise was clothed in secrecy. As has been noted, whalers were expected to become insane; insanity, in the Aleut order of things, was considered an inevitable consequence of sins committed in secret.

Linguistically, whales were distinguished as a class (*Alan*). In the Eastern Aleutians twelve species of dolphin and whales were named. In the Central Aleutians, the number of specific names was much lower (Veniaminov 1840; Netsvetov 1980). The anatomical characteristics of whales were very well understood; one of the first scientific descriptions of the Pacific whales (after Steller and Pallas in the eighteenth century) was based on detailed information and wooden models made specifically for the purpose by Unalaskan Aleuts in 1818 (Chamisso 1825). The whales, as a class, were grouped neither with sea mammals (who were grouped together in an unnamed class on the basis of the criterion of hauling out on shore) nor with fishes. The Aleuts apparently conceptualized whales as very special creatures of the sea, fishlike in appearance, but very different from fish in general (my field data). In the available recorded folklore, conceptualization of whales is not explicitly expressed. As far as I can tell, they were not conceptualized as sea monsters (though stories about sea monsters are known to have existed), and Elliott's (1882) vague reference to such conceptualization is, in my opinion, not warranted.

It is not clear if the whale was associated with notions of the evil principle. However, the whale *hunt* was in some way so associated. Iokhel'son (Ms.) recorded two tales in which whale hunting is mentioned, and in both instances Man, in order to be able to hunt whales, had to associate himself with evil forces, represented in one instance by the raven (Attu, in the Western Aleutians), and in the second by the killer whale (Eastern Aleutians).

Moreover, whale hunting was linked with death, or more precisely, with a special class of the dead, either whale hunters or perhaps powerful shamans of the past, whose bodies were preserved in secret caves (mummies interred in a special manner). The Aleuts call such "dead ones" or "the ancient ones" *asxaanas* (Atka dialect) or *asxaagin* (eastern dialect). A would-be hunter had to put himself in touch, by actual physical contact, with the *asxaagin* to derive the needed, but very dangerous, power. Veniaminov's description of rites associated with whale hunting supports the notion that the hunter, though he became powerful, also became contaminated and, in a sense, carried within him a germ of death: the use of magical substances prepared from the fat or other tissues of corpses and applied to the hunter's person, weapons, and kayak was a very prominent feature of all whale hunting rituals. The hunter struck the whale only once and then immediately returned to shore, where he commenced a period of isolation. This period lasted normally four days, but could be terminated earlier if the whale carcass was washed ashore. The hunter remained alone in a special structure of the same type as the huts constructed for menstruating women. It is significant that after the hunter's isolation ended, he rejoined human society only after undergoing rites of purification.[11]

It is possible to interpret the available information by postulating that the whale hunter offered himself to evil power and courted death in the service of his community. Such "dedication to death" would be consistent with Aleut ideals. Specifically, it would be consistent with the explicit tenet that an Aleut should defend his community unto death and face "natural" death— that is, death in war or hunt—unflinchingly. An Aleut was expected to go forward to meet death in battle. Similarly, criminals condemned to death were expected to go forward to meet their executioners. (The latter behavior pattern was recorded in very recent times [Wheaton 1945].) Whales were not associated with "unnatural" death—that is, death from such causes as disease.

Thus, the two animals stressed in the Aleut precontact world view—the sea otter and the whale—were not, and could not have been, conceptualized in precontact time as potentially disease-causing agents. The precontact conceptualization of these species does not permit even their redefinition, under changed postcontact circumstances, as disease-causing agents. That no such redefinition occurred is evidenced by the history of these species being taken by the Aleuts in postcontact times.

Conversion to Christianity

In the Aleut area, conversion to Christianity preceded the depletion of species by better than a century. Martin generalizes the process of conversion of various Indian groups to Christianity and projects a single continent-wide model of this process. He describes the effect of conversion to this undifferentiated Christianity as follows: "No longer was he [the Micmac] the sensitive fellow-member of a symbolic world; under pressure from disease, European trade, and Christianity, he had apostatized—he had repudiated his role within the ecosystem" (p. 61); "Christianity furnished a new, dualistic world view, lending spiritual support to the fur trade by elevating man above Nature and making the hunt profane" (p. 65). Elsewhere he quotes approvingly from the dissertation by Adrian Tanner: "Hunters go forth from the lodge, the *soiled human realm*, to the bush, the clean spirit realm" (p. 114; my emphasis).

This schema does not apply to the Aleuts on several counts. Aside from the fact that, to my knowledge, all people make a conceptual distinction between human and animal domains, Aleuts, in common with many other human groups, regarded the human sphere as orderly by nature; by nature it was in harmony with the source of universal power, the bond being eternal and immutable, "good." The notion that *orderly* human society could be "soiled" was foreign to the Aleuts. Pollution came from outside, from "the bush," where uncontrolled forces could work their evil ways. And even then, these forces, as

131

mentioned in the earlier sections of this paper, could enter the human realm only if humans themselves violated the natural order of things through sin, through moral transgressions. These outside evil influences manifested themselves in illness and absence of important prey animals. Thus, in the Aleut theory of causation it was ultimately the human agency, perhaps inspired or possessed by the uncontrolled forces of "the bush," that was responsible for disorder (disease, the "bad death" through disease, scarcity, etc.). Hence, there was a need for shamans to assign blame and prescribe the remedy—usually, rites of exorcism and apotropy. In severe cases, restitution of order was effected through punishment of the transgressors, either real or identified as such by a shaman, and by purification of the entire community.

Christianity did not introduce dualism, in the sense that Martin writes about, into the Aleut world view. Aleut concepts were dualistic to begin with, and Christianity, if anything, attenuated the preexisting dualism. The Christianity the Aleuts adopted soon after contact was not the unitary entity so simplistically presented in much of anthropological literature and described by Martin as an antithesis of all other religious beliefs. As in any successful conversion situation, there was a considerable overlap between the ideological notions of the Aleuts and those of the bearers of the new Orthodox Christianity.[12] Both held many beliefs in common, both were in agreement as to the function of religion, and both groups (as all people do) came to terms with the conditions of material existence through the use of a symbolic system. It was an historical accident that there was also a considerable overlap between the two symbolic systems. In the end, the symbolic system of the Aleuts became integrated with the symbolic system of the intruders, and the Orthodox Church became an identity marker of Aleut people (Berreman 1955; Jones as cited; Black 1977). The basic premises of the Aleut belief system were perceived to be congenial with the belief system of the Russians. In sum, the process of syncretism was at work. Syncretism, especially in popular usage, is often perceived in derogatory terms. In reality, syncretism, inevitable in almost any contact situation, is a vital process, an adaptive mechanism of humanity. It is a special case of ideological change. Ideologies, like cultures, are dynamic systems which change over time as man reflects upon conditions of his existence. In the words of a theologian (for lack of anthropological theory on the subject), "Human existence is a thinking existence. Man makes himself by thinking his life . . . development is inevitable and necessary because the expression of faith is human and . . . all manifestations of man are characterized by historicity" (Walgrave 1972:3, 332).

Seldom, if ever, is there complete replacement. The paradox of culture, which provides both for continuity and change (Bock 1973), holds for ideological systems also. An ideology provides the system of orientation for any individual and as such must maintain links to the past as it helps one to face the future: "Man lives in view of the past. *Man in a word, has no nature; what he has is . . . history*" (Ortega y Gasset 1961:217; emphasis in original). The "death" or "loss" of a culture is a myth, as is the notion of ideological purity, which has no more reality than the myth of "pure race."

Anthropological theory is sadly deficient in its analysis of ideological change, syncretism, and conversion. Here, I define conversion as the consciously articulated and perceived change of explicitly stated assumptions and premises relative to human existence. There is often a concomitant change in symbols used to encode, for purposes of communication, these assumptions and premises (*inter alia*, Coulanges 1956; Durkheim 1965). As stated previously, this process is facilitated if there is an overlap between the two systems of belief and symbols impinging onto the consciousness of individuals. I maintain that this overlap is a significant factor in the differential success of various missionaries, Christian and otherwise. The overlap need not be clearly articulated: it need only be intuitively experienced, so that recoding of basic assumptions in the new symbolic vehicles is possible.

Such was the case in the Aleutians. Today, Orthodoxy is perceived as *the* Aleut church, both by natives and nonnatives alike. A taped statement by a nonnative informant, a member of a Protestant denomination, holds that "the Orthodox church is not a Christian church; it is a native religion, the native superstition." This sentiment was widely shared by government officials who dealt with the Aleuts in various capacities, from the managers of the Pribilof Islands' fur-sealing operation, who objected to Aleuts' "wasting their money" for church candles, to Methodist and later Bureau of Indian Affairs teachers (West 1938). There was an attempt to eradicate Orthodoxy on the grounds that it was a "native superstition," vaguely un-American, and detrimental to the native's "progress" and assimilation to the larger American society (see, e.g., Birkeland 1926). Martin assumes "Christianity" to be synonymous with "missionization," by which he means the conscious introduction, sometimes by force, of a new ideology by specialists. This did not occur in the Aleutians. The first resident priest arrived in the Eastern Aleutians in 1825 (Veniaminov), and the very first priest even to visit the Western Aleutians (Netsvetov) came in 1829—almost a century after contact. Both found the populace calling themselves Christians. All had been baptized by laymen. In their activities, both priests were aided by prominent Aleuts (Veniaminov 1840; Black 1977; Netsvetov 1980). The memory of Veniaminov, now Saint Innocent of the Aleutians, is revered to this day (see Aleut for Beginners 1975 : 33). Netsvetov, himself an Aleut, is remembered as a leader and an intellectual (my field data).

By whom, then, were the Aleuts Christianized? Who were the men who carried Orthodoxy to Alaska? They were peasants from Northern Russia, Siberian natives of various ethnic origins, and adventurers from remote regions of the Empire—a Greek, an Armenian, a Jew. They were familiar with the lifestyle of the Aleuts, having hunted for decades in Siberia and the Aleutians, and having traded and warred with various groups both in Asia and in Alaska. They readily adopted modes of

Aleut dress, native tools and weapons, housing and food, recognizing technical excellence, functional utility, and superior local environmental knowledge when they saw it. They had a healthy respect for the natives' ability to cope with the environment, and they were learning from the natives even as they were engaged with them in armed conflict. Many chose to settle among the Aleuts.

Their concept of the function of religion was not far from that of the Aleuts. They, like the Aleuts, looked to their faith to avert misfortune and help one over the rough spots in life, principally in the hour of death. Like the Aleuts, they believed in the power of symbols and in the power of ritual action. They were not bookish people. Like the Aleuts, they carried their own talismans and had their own personal protectors, the saints whose aid they invoked. They believed in a special link to their name saint and to the saint of their locality—that is, the saint to whom they dedicated the chapels they built. Specifically, they believed in the power of religion to cure. As late as the 1820s, Aleut shamans were active as curers throughout the chain, and the "Old Voyagers" used the shamans' services in much the same way as Aleuts, since the 1750s, had used baptism to cure those who were pronounced incurable by their own (see, for example, Andreyev 1948).[13] Many, like the Aleuts, believed that the future could be known and that men with ritual power could change things. Members of both groups engaged in ritual preparation for the hunt, as Stepan Cherepanov, who eventually spent nearly fifty years in the Aleutians, reported:

As we Russians call and invoke the name of God, our Lord, whenever we commence any activity, and call [upon him] to come to our aid and bless [our enterprises] or when we set out to hunt on the sea to hunt in our baidaras and observe a silence and then say "God aid us," so these foreign peoples also, commencing the hunt say a prayer like "Lord bless." The same when they travel in baidaras just like us, they call out "God will aid us." They are very understanding of the Orthodox Christian faith and do not doubt that we possess the truth. [In Andreyev 1948:117–18; my translation]

The custom of ritual preparation for hunting or other important enterprises was not abandoned with conversion to Christianity and has been maintained to modern times. As late as the end of the nineteenth century, Aleut hunters prepared for the walrus hunt by prayer, fasting, ablutions, and the donning of a clean shirt—the last, a Russian custom, observed when facing mortal danger (Kashevarov-Yanovskiy correspondence 1862: 90). It is reported that in earlier times Aleuts who went out on the walrus hunt prayed, fasted, and took leave of each other as if about to die (Khlebnikov 1979). Fasting (including sexual abstinence) is an important ritual activity of the Orthodox even today. As late as 1912–13 Aleuts refused to proceed aboard whaling vessels at Akutan without proper ritual preparation and, to that end, held a special church service (Birkeland 1926:79–85).

Gordon H. Marsh, discussing the Eskimo and Aleut religious systems, defined these as "primarily pragmatic systems for treating with the forces of nature and only secondarily a system of explaining causes and origins" (1954:35). In the same article he wrote: "Eskimo-Aleut religion comprises a set of beliefs about the supernatural plus a body of public and a body of private rituals for dealing therewith. It provides its practitioners with an essentially pragmatic system for treating the forces of nature so as to control the weather and the food supply, to ensure protection against harm and disease, to provide a means of curing sickness and disorders, and prognosticate coming events" (1954:21). This characterization could just as easily be applied to the pragmatic, practical everyday religiosity of Russian imperial citizens who came to the Aleutians in the eighteenth century and who listed first on their ships' manifests the icons and crosses which symbolized their faith (Makarova 1968). If the Aleuts were people of a symbolic world, so were the Russian citizens who came into the Aleut domain, and their symbols had much in common. Both groups prayed to the East; symbolized the creative, benevolent principle with the sky and light; shared the ritual numbers three, seven, and forty; believed in ritual purification and confession of sins (Netsvetov 1980); had symbols to protect home and territory; believed in the life-giving, cleansing, and restorative powers of water; believed in the power of the name to establish a link between the human and supernatural domains; and valued the right above the left.

To sum up, while the dogma of Orthodoxy could not be directly compared to any known Aleut dogma, the Aleuts and the Russians shared mutual understanding with respect to the function of religion and the value of symbols and ritual actions, as well as basic premises, the *eidos*, underlying their belief systems. Conversion was speedy, voluntary, and permanent long before the arrival of the first priest and even longer before the fur bearers became depleted.

As far as one can judge on the basis of available evidence, conversion to Christianity had no effect whatsoever on the Aleut perception of the hunt, on their hunting practices, or on the number of animals they killed. If anything, conversion to Orthodoxy became their chief adaptive mechanism and the vehicle for maintenance of ethnic identity.

On the other hand, a clear and unmistakable connection between the development of the market economy, new hunting technology, and unregulated hunting of fur-bearing species by outsiders, and the depletion—even near-extermination—of important species can be demonstrated. This connection was recognized by the Aleuts themselves, as is evident from the petition which they addressed to President Cleveland in 1886 and which is presented as an appendix to this chapter.

The Aleuts feared the decrease of the valuable sea animals they hunted; they feared the supremacy and economic competition of "the whites." They did not fear the sea animals; they did not at any time believe the animals to be agents of disease and misfortune, and had no desire to exterminate them. Aleuts knew then, as they had known since time immemorial, and as they know today, that animals were indispensable to their survival.

Appendix

Ounalaska, Alaska ter., April 19th 1886
His Excellency Grover Cleveland
   President of the United States
     Washington, D.C.

Sir:

We, the undersigned natives of Alaska have the honor to send you the following petition and trust that our prayer for relief will not pass unheeded.

Under the provisions of section 1955 Revised Statutes the importation of firearms and ammunition is prohibited, permission is however granted to white hunters who marry native women, also to immigrants actual settlers and residents to import for their own use breech-loading arms and suitable ammunition into all parts of Alaska including its islands, with the exception of the Pribilof Islands.

We gain our daily bread by the chase. Our principle occupation is sea otter hunting.

Many years ago when these animals were plentiful we were enabled to hunt them successfully with spears. Gradually white hunters settled amongst us, these having superior fire-arms, forced us also to change our mode of hunting, and we were supplied with muzzle-loading fire-arms.

The white hunters have since erected their dwellings on islands and islets, the hauling grounds and resting places of the sea otter, which is a very shy and sensitive animal.

This deplorable practice if permitted to continue will soon force them to desert these places and our hunting grounds.

They are now disappearing from some localities and search for still more unapproachable places.

And hence badly armed and having to battle with our increasing difficulties and dangers in the persuit [*sic*] of our daily avocation.

We beg respectfully that the permission granted to other hunters to import breech-loading rifles, but withheld from us, be also extended to us, and thus enable us to gain our subsistence by our own exertion.

Also that nobody should be permitted to build and inhabit any dwellings on the hauling and resting places of the sea otter, and section 1956 Revised Statu[t]es prohibiting the killing of fur-bearing animals without the consent of the Secretary of the Treasury. [one line unreadable] be strictly enforced, as well as penalties against violating this law by vessels.

[Follow 240 individual signatures] [14]

Notes

In the course of fieldwork I incurred many debts. I hereby acknowledge, with gratitude, the help given me by members of the Aleut communities of Iliulliuk (Unalaska), Nikol'ski (Unnak), Akutan, St. Paul, and St. George (the Pribilof Islands): Mr. Henry Swanson, Mrs. E. Pelageia McCurdy, Mr. Agafangel Steptin, Mr. and Mrs. Sergel Suvoroff, Mr. and Mrs. Arthur Stepetin, Mr. Philimon Tutiakoff, Mr. Vasiliy Cherepanoff, Mr. and Mrs. Vasiliy Ermeloff, Father and Mrs. Islail Gromoff, and Father and Mrs. Paul Merculief. I am very grateful to Mr. Ray Hudson, of Unalaska, my host for a season of fieldwork, who put at my disposal copies of the petition of the Aleuts to President Cleveland and documents relating to it, which he located in the archives of the University of Alaska, Fairbanks.

I thank my colleagues Thomas E. Lux and Rafael van Kets,

both of Providence College, and Dwight B. Heath, Brown University, who read preliminary drafts of this paper and especially Douglas D. Anderson, Brown University, who critically read the final draft.

1. The literature on the conceptualization of animals is enormous, and a growing body of works address themselves to specific ways in which the human-animal relationship is conceptualized specifically among groups with hunting subsistence. For a partial listing of sources see Black 1973. Jensen (1951; Eng. trans. 1963) discussed the concept of Masters of Animals in general and global perspective. Very useful is Burgmann 1968 and Virsaladze 1973, which contains additional citations. Zerries 1954 and Reichel-Dolmatoff 1971 and 1975 provide both useful discussion and excellent references.

2. Early Russian skippers' reports on linguistic and cultural differences between various Aleut groups find support in archaeological data. McCartney 1971 postulated a divergent cultural development for the Western Aleutians.

3. The most widely published population estimate, 16,000–19,000, used as a base by William S. Laughlin and his students, originated as an educated guess by Mooney (1929) that was later elaborated by Kroeber (1963). Mooney's data for Alaska were scant, to say the least (Ubelaker 1976). Current population estimates are also mostly guesswork, and some postulated densities appear fantastically high (as for example Harper's estimate of 4.6 persons per coastal mile or 64.7 per 100 sq km, cited by Yesner 1977:21). Most specialists (Lantis 1970; McCartney 1975) tend to considerably lower estimates for the total population, ranging from 5,000 to 12,000.

4. Not all of the following epidemics occurred throughout the entire Aleutian settlement area: 1789, infection manifest through pulmonary symptoms (Merck 1937); 1805–1806, pulmonary and intestinal infection in Eastern Aleutians

(Khlebnikov 1979); 1808, possibly the same infection carried by a vessel to the Western Aleutians (Vasil'yev 1823); 1807, intestinal infection in the Eastern Aleutians; 1830–31, in the Eastern Aleutians, and not in all communities, a pulmonary infection (Veniaminov 1840); 1831–32, an intestinal infection with unusually high mortality in the Western Aleutians (Netsvetov, in press). In later years, the occurrence of epidemic diseases becomes rare, and the gross birth statistics exceed the gross death statistics, so that a small but steady population increase is manifest for several decades (Black, work in progress).

5. On Aleut belief system see Marsh 1954; Lantis 1938, 1940 addendum, 1947; Heizer 1938, 1943a, 1943b; and Veniaminov 1840. The sources for Aleut folklore are Veniaminov 1840, Netsvetov (in Veniaminov 1840, 3:20–26), Golder (as cited), Iokhel'son (as cited), and Elliott 1882.

6. *Creole*, as used in the Russian context, indicated a civil status roughly equivalent to that of a townsman or burgher in Russia itself. Persons claiming at least one Russian citizen as ancestor or ancestress were designated creoles regardless of genealogical distance from the said ancestor/ancestress. Creoles had special privileges and rights, especially with regard to education, not available to Russians of comparable social status and, consequently, were often resented by Russian employees in Alaska. After 1867, this group —which provided Russian America with navigators, skippers, teachers, priests, and managers—suffered a tremendous psychological trauma when they were reclassified as "half-breeds." Many became reabsorbed into Aleut communities and came to identify themselves as Aleuts; others developed the art of "passing," not unlike the light-skinned blacks of the times.

7. There is some evidence that conservation practices were followed, at least occasionally, even earlier. Sometime between the late 1790s and 1805 Maxim Lazarev moved the Amchitkans to Atka in order to "rest" the Amchitka sea

otter banks. Peter Corney, who sailed the Aleutian waters in 1816, presumably poaching off the Pribilofs, reports that only "last year's pups" were killed by the Russians (Corney 1897:51). A full halt to the fur seal kill in the Pribilofs was ordered by Banner, Baranov's deputy, in 1806. Sea otters were protected by control of settlement as well as by hunting regulations. Between 1823 and 1826 the population of Sannak in the Eastern Aleutians was moved to the Alaskan Peninsula, where the village of Belkofsky was built, to protect the Sannak sea otter hauling grounds. See Hooper 1897 for the best description of sea otter conservation measures, and also Alaska Journal 1893.

8. For the methods and effects of pelagic sealing see King 1964 and Bering Sea Tribunal 1897, 3:187–229. For an eyewitness account of pelagic sealing see Morell 1832. On sea otter depletion see Hooper 1897 and, outside Alaska, Ogden 1975. See also Hall 1945, Lensink 1960, Kenyon 1975, and the work of Chase Littlejohn (not cited here). For the effect on sea otter hunting of the introduction of the repeating and breech-loading rifles, see, in addition to Hooper, the Aleut petition to President Cleveland reprinted in the Appendix, above.

9. Today, sea otters have recovered and are eating themselves out of house and home. When the herd becomes too large for the feeding ground to support, it is culled by Fish and Wildlife personnel and the pelts are sold on the international market, the revenue accruing to the State of Alaska (Kenyon 1975). The Aleuts, of course, are prohibited from taking any sea otter, a protected species. Besides, the Aleuts have by now lost the necessary skills, and the majority lack the necessary equipment, such as seaworthy boats.

10. After 1826, only nonbreeding males from three to five years old, the "bachelors," were taken.

11. On the other hand, it is possible to interpret this purification as an indication that the hunter, through contact,

became imbued with superhuman power incarnated in the whale and thus became dangerous for his fellow men. Purification, in this case, may be seen as sloughing off this excess power. It should also be noted that whale hunters, in addition to using corpse substances as talismans, also used menstrual matter, otherwise shunned and feared by all males.

12. I use the term *ideology*, following Bock 1973, in the sense of a broad system of orientation, encompassing explicit and implicit socially defined systems of belief and values.

13. Aleut shamans possessed excellent anatomical knowledge and used an extensive pharmacopoeia (Veniaminov 1840, 2:259–62; Laughlin and Marsh 1951:85–86).

14. This petition is taken from a photocopy put at my disposal by Ray Hudson, Unalaska, who located the original in the archives of the University of Alaska, Fairbanks. He did not complete the photocopying of the signatures, but made a note that the original petition was signed by 240 Aleut hunters. The petition was written by Father Nikolay Rysef, a native of Unalaska, who soon after was transferred to a subordinate parish.

References Cited

Alaska Journal
   1893   Sea Otter Hunting. Alaska Journal, vol. 1, no. 10, May 6.
Aleut for Beginners
   1975   Prepared for the use of Unalaska City School, Unalaska, Aleut Language Instruction, by Fr. Ismail Gromoff in collaboration with Sergei Suvoroff of Nikol'ski, Umnak, and Vasiliy Cherepanoff of

Akutan. With assistance of Mr. Ray Hudson. Published by Unalaska City School, Aleut Language Program.

Andreyev, A. I., ed.
1948   Russkiye otkrytiya v Tikhom Okeane i Severn Amerike v XVIII–XIX vekakh (Russian Discoveries in the Pacific and North America in the 18th–19th Centuries). Moscow and Leningrad: Akademiya Nauk USSR.

Bergsland, Knut
1959   Aleut Dialects of Atka and Attu. Transactions of the American Philosophical Society, vol. 49, no. 3.
1979   Niigugis Maqaxtazaqangis. Atkan Historical Traditions told in 1952 by Cedor L. Snigaroff. 2nd ed., corrected and revised by K. Bergsland and M. Dirks. Fairbanks: Alaska Native Language Center, University of Alaska.

Bering Sea Tribunal of Arbitration
1895   Fur seal arbitration Proceedings of the Tribunal convened at Paris under the treaty between the United States and Great Britain concluded at Washington February 29, 1892, for the determination of questions between the two governments concerning the jurisdiction of the United States in the Waters of the Bering Sea. Executive Documents of the United States for the Second Session of the Fifty-Third Congress, No. 3166. 16 vols. Washington, D.C.: Government Printing Office.

Berremen, Gerald D.
1955   Inquiry into Community Integration in an Aleut Village. American Anthropologist 57:49–59.

Birkeland, Knut B.
1926   The Whalers of Akutan: An Account of Modern Whaling in the Aleutian Islands. New Haven: Yale University Press.

Black, Lydia T.
1973   Dogs, Bears and Killer Whales: Analysis of the

Nivkh Symbolic System. Ph.D. dissertation, University of Massachusetts, Amherst.

1977   Ivan Pan'kov: An Architect of Aleut Literacy. Arctic Archaeology 14(1):94–107.

Blaschke, E.

1848   Neskol'ko Zamechanly o plavaniyi v baydarkakh i o Lis'yevskikh Aleutakh (Several Remarks about Navigation in Baidarkas and the Fox Island Aleuts). Morskoy Sbornik 1:115–24, 160–65.

Bock, Philip D.

1973   Modern Cultural Anthropology. 2nd ed. New York: Knopf.

Burgmann, Arno

1968   Neue Forschungen ueber den "Herrn der Tiere." Paper presented at the VIII International Congress of Anthropological and Ethnological Sciences. Tokyo & Kyoto, September 3–10, 1968.

Chamisso, Adelbertus de

1825   Cetaceorum maris Kamtschatici imagines ab Aleutis e ligno fictas. . . . Nova Acts Physico-Medica, Academiae Caesarae Leopoldino-Carolinae Naturae Curiosorum Bonn.

Chandler, Joan M.

1974   Anthropological Perspectives on Southwestern Indians, 1928–1966. Paper presented at the Seventy-third Annual Meeting of the American Anthropological Association, Mexico City, November 22–24, 1974.

Corney, Peter

1897   Voyages in the North Pacific. . . . Honolulu: Thomas C. Trum.

Coulanges, Fustel des

1956   The Ancient City. Garden City, N.Y.: Doubleday.

Durkheim, Emile

1965   The Elementary Forms of the Religious Life. New York: Free Press.

Ellicott, Henry W., ed.
1882   An Alaska Legend. Continent 2(1):5–8.

Fassett, H. D.
1890   The Aleut Sea Otter Hunt in the Late Nineteenth
        Century. San Francisco Chronicle, December 28,
        1890. *Reprinted in* Anthropological Papers of the
        University of Alaska, May 1960, 8(2):131–35, ed.
        Robert F. Heizer.

Federova, Svetlana G.
1979   Shturmany Ivany Vasil'yevy i ikh rol v izucheniyi
        Alyaski (Navigators Ivans Vasilyev and Their Role
        in the Study of Alaska). Vol. 9, pp. 167–210, Mos-
        cow: Mysl'.

Geertz, Clifford
1965   Religion as a Cultural System. *In* Anthropological
        Approaches to the Study of Religion, ed. Michael
        Banton, pp. 1–46. London: Tavistock.

Golder, Frank A.
1905   Aleutian Stories. Journal of American Folklore
        18(70):215–22.
1907   The Songs and Stories of the Aleuts, with Transla-
        tions from Veniaminov. Journal of American
        Folklore 20(76):132–42.
1909a   Eskimo and Aleut Stories from Alaska. Journal of
        American Folklore 22:10–24.
1909b   Primitive Warfare among the Natives of Western
        Alaska. Journal of American Folklore 22:336–39.

Hall, Raymond E.
1945   Chase Littlejohn, 1854–1943: Observations by Lit-
        tlejohn on Hunting Sea Otter. Journal of Mammol-
        ogy 26(1):89–91.

Heizer, Robert F.
1938   Aconite Arrow Poison in the Old and New World.
        Washington Academy of Science Journal
        28(8):358–64.
1943a   Aconite Poison Whaling in Asia and America: An

Aleutian Transfer to the New World. Smithsonian Institution, Bureau of American Ethnology, Bulletin 133, Anthropological Papers, No. 24. Washington, D.C.: Government Printing Office.

1943*b*   A Pacific Eskimo Invention in Whale Hunting in Historic Times. American Anthropologist 45:120–22.

Hooper, Calvin L.

1897   A Report on the Sea Otter Banks of Alaska: Range and Habits of the Sea Otter—Its Decrease under American Rule, and Some of Its Causes—Importance of the Sea Otter to the Natives of Alaska, Inhabitants of the Aleutian Islands. Proposed Regulations for 1898. U.S. Treasury Documents, No. 1977, U.S. Revenue Cutter Service, Office of the Secretary. Washington, D.C.: Government Printing Office.

Iokhel'son, Vladimir (Jochelson, Waldemar)

1915   Obraztsy Materialov po Aleutskoy Zhivoy Starine (Examples of Materials from the Aleutian Living Past). Zhivaya Starina 3:293–308.

1923   Materialy po izucheniyu aleutskogo yazka i folklora: Teksty na Unalashkinskom narechiyi (Materials for the Study of the Aleutian Language: Texts in Unalaska Dialect). Vol. 1, no. 1. Petrograd: Akademia Nauk.

1933   History, Ethnology, and Anthropology of the Aleut. Washington, D.C.: Carnegie Institution.

1934   Unanganaskiy (Aleutskiy) yazyk (Unangan [Aleutian] Language). *In* Yazyki i pis'mennost' narodov Severa (Languages and Writing Systems of the Peoples of the North), ed. Ya. P. Al'kor, pp. 139–48. Moscow and Leningrad: Gosudarstvennoye uchebnopedagogicheskoye izdatel'stvo.

Ms.   Waledmar Jochhelson Papers, Aleutian Series, Aleutian Ms. Deposit, New York Public Library.

Jensen, A. D.
1951   Mythos und Kult bei Naturevoelkern. Wiesbaden:
          Franz Steiner Verlag. (English translation 1963.
          Myth and Cult among Primitive Peoples, trans.
          M. T. Choldin and W. Eeissleder. Chicago: Univer-
          sity of Chicago Press.)

Jones, Dorothy M.
1969   A Study of Social and Economic Problems in Un-
          alaska, an Aleut Village. Ph.D. dissertation, Uni-
          versity of California.

1970   Changes in the Population Structure of the Aleu-
          tian Islands. Fairbanks: Institute of Social, Eco-
          nomic, and Governmental Research, University of
          Alaska.

1972a   Adaptations of Whites in an Alaskan Native Vil-
          lage. Anthropologica 14(2): 199–218.

1972b   Contemporary Aleut Material Culture. In Modern
          Alaskan Native Culture, ed. W. Oswalt, pp. 7–19.
          College, Alaska: University of Alaska Museum.

1973a   Race Relations in an Alaskan Village. Anthropo-
          logica 15(2): 167–90.

1973b   Patterns of Village Growth and Decline. Fairbanks:
          Institute of Social, Economic, and Governmental
          Research, Occasional Paper No. 11, October 1973.
          Fairbanks: University of Alaska.

1974   The Urban-Native Encounter. Fairbanks: Institute of
          Social, Economic, and Governmental Research,
          University of Alaska.

Kashevarov-Yanovskiy Correspondence
1861–62   "Chto takoye zapusk" (What is Zapusk-stoppage of
          kill). Morskoy Sbornik (1861), 7 (appendix): 18–20;
          1–10; and ibid. (1862), 4:86–92, 9:152–68, 6
          (appendix): 1–8.

Kenyon, Karl W.
1975   The Sea Otter in the Eastern Pacific Ocean. New
          York: Dover.

Khlebnikov, Kiril T.
1979   Russkaya America v neopublikovannykh zapiskakh
        Khlebnikova (Russian America from Unpublished
        Notes by Khlebnikov). Compiled, annotated, and
        with an introduction by R. G. Liapunova and S. G.
        Fedorova. Leningrad: Nauka.

King, Judith E.
1964   Seals of the World. London: Trustees of the British
        Museum. Natural History.

Kroeber, A. L.
1963   Cultural and Natural Areas of Native North Amer-
        ica. Berkeley: University of California Press.

Lantis, Margaret
1938   The Alaskan Whale Cult and Its Affinities. Ameri-
        can Anthropoligist 40:438-64.
1940   Note on the Alaskan Whale Cult and Its Affinities.
        American Anthropologist 42:366-68.
1947   Alaskan Eskimo Ceremonialism. Monographs of
        the American Ethnological Society, No. 2.
1970   The Aleut Social System, 1750 to 1810, from Early
        Historical Sources. In Ethnohistory in Southwest-
        ern Alaska and the Southern Yukon: Method and
        Content, ed. M. Lantis, pp. 139-301. Lexington:
        University Press of Kentucky.

Laughlin, William S., and Jean S. Aigner
1975   Aleut Adaptation and Evolution. In Prehistoric
        Maritime Adaptations of the Circumpolar Zone, ed.
        William Fitzhugh, pp. 181-201. The Hague:
        Mouton.

Laughlin, William S., and Gordon Marsh
1951   A New View of the History of the Aleutians. Arctic
        4(2):75-88.

Lensink, Calvin
1960   Sea Otter in Alaska. Journal of Mammology 41(2):
        172-82.

Liapunova, Roza G.

1979   Novyi dokument o rannikh plavaniyakh na Aleu-
         tskiye ostrova: Izvestiya' Fedora Afanas'yevicha
         Kul'kova 1764 g (New Document Pertaining to
         Early Voyages to the Aleutians: "News" by Fedor
         A. Kul'kov, 1764). *In* Strany i narody Vostoka
         (Countries and Peoples of the East), vol. 20, book 4,
         Strany i narody basseyna Tikhogo Okeana (Coun-
         tries and Peoples of the Pacific Ocean), pp. 97–105.
         Moscow: Nauka.

McCartney, Allen P.

1971   A Proposed Western Aleutian Phase in the Near Is-
         lands, Alaska. Arctic Anthropology 8(2):92–142.

1975   Maritime Adaptations in Cold Archipelagos. *In* Pre-
         historic Adapations of the Circumpolar Zone, ed.
         William Fitzhugh, pp. 281–338. The Hague:
         Mouton.

Makarova, Raisa V.

1968   Russkiye na Tikhom Okeane vo vtoroy polovine
         XVIIIv. Moscow: Nauka. (English translation 1975.
         Russians on the Pacific, 1743–1799, trans. R. A.
         Pierce and A. Donnelly. Kingston, Ont.: The Lime-
         stone Press.)

Mannheim, Karl

1936   Ideology and Utopia: An Introduction to the Sociol-
         ogy of Knowledge. New York: Harcourt, Brace and
         World.

Marsh, Gordon H.

1954   A Comparative Survey of Eskimo-Aleut Religion.
         Anthropological Papers of the University of Alaska
         3(1):21–36.

Martin, Calvin

1978   Keepers of the Game: Indian-Animal Relationships
         and the Fur Trade. Berkeley: University of Califor-
         nia Press.

Merck, Carl Heinrich
1937   Beobachtungen ueber Voelker des Beringmeeres,
        1789–1791: Nach seinem Tagebuche bearbeitet von
        A. Jocobi. *In* Basler Archiv 1937: 113–37.

Mooney, James
1929   The Aboriginal Population of America North of
        Mexico. Smithsonian Miscellaneous Collections,
        vol. 80, no. 7. Washington, D.C.: Government Print-
        ing Office.

Morrell, Benjamin, Jr.
1832   A Narrative of Four Voyages, to the South Sea,
        North and South Pacific Ocean, Chinese Sea, Ethi-
        opic and Southern Atlantic Ocean, Indian and
        Arctic Ocean from the Year 1822–1831. . . . New
        York: J. & J. Harper.

Murie, Olaus J.
1959   Fauna of the Aleutian Island and with Notes on the
        Alaska Peninsula. With notes on Invertebrates and
        Fish Collected in the Aleutians, 1936–38, by Victor
        B. Scheffer, Biologist. North American Fauna, No.
        61. U.S. Department of the Interior, Fish and Wild-
        life Service.

Netsvetov, Yakov
1980   The Journals of Yakov Netsvetov: The Atkha Years,
        1828–1843. L. Black, trans. and ed. Kingston, Ont.:
        The Limestone Press.

Ogden, Adele
1975   The California Sea Otter Trade, 1784–1848.
        Berkeley: University of California Press.

Ortega y Gasset, José
1961   History as a System and Other Essays toward a Phi-
        losophy of History. New York: Norton.

Powdermaker, Hortense
1966   Stranger and Friend: The Way of an Anthropolo-
        gist. New York: Norton.

Russian American Company
Ms.   Records. Correspondence of Governors General, 92
         vols. U.S. National Archives, Washington, D.C. Mi-
         crofilm Publication No. 11.
Redfield, Robert
1953   The Primitive World and Its Transformations.
         Ithaca, N.Y.: Cornell University Press.
Reichel-Dolmatoff, Gerardo
1971   Amazonian Cosmos: The Sexual and Religious
         Symbolism of the Tukano Indians. Chicago: Univer-
         sity of Chicago Press.
1975   The Shaman and the Jaguar: A Study of Narcotic
         Drugs among the Indians of Colombia. Phila-
         delphia: Temple University Press.
Sarychev, Gavrilo
1802   Puteshestviye Flota Kapitana Sarycheva po sever-
         ovostochnov chasti Sibiri, Ledovitomu moriu i
         Vostochnomu okeana, v prodolzheniyi os'mi let pri
         Geograficheskoy i Astronomicheskoy Morskoy
         Ekspeditsiyi, byyshey pod nachal'stvom Flota Ka-
         pitana Billingsa 1785 po 1793 god. (The voyage of
         Captain Sarychev through northeastern Siberia, the
         Arctic Sea, and the Eastern Ocean, lasting eight
         years and undertaken in connection with the Geo-
         graphic and Astronomic Naval Expedition under
         command of Captain Billings in the years 1785–
         1793). St. Petersburg: Schnor.
Scammon, C.
1870   The Sea Otter. The American Naturalist 4(2):65–74.
Tikhmenev, P. A.
1978   A History of the Russian-American Company.
         Richard A. Pierce and A. Donnelly, trans. and eds.
         Seattle: University of Washington Press.
Ubelaker, Douglas H.
1976   The Sources and Methodology for Mooney's Esti-
         mates of North American Indian Population. In The
         Native Populations of the Americas, ed. William M.

Denevan, pp. 243–88. Madison: University of
Wisconsin Press.

Vasil'yev, Ivan
 1823   Vypiski iz puteshestviya shturmana Vasil'yeva,
         Ivana Filipovocha na sudne *Finlandia* 1811–12 g, v
         Aleutskikh ostrovakh (Extracts from the Account of
         a Voyage by the Navigator Vasil'yev, Ivan F., on the
         Vessel *Finlandia* in the Years 1811–12 in the Aleu-
         tian Islands). Novosti Literatury 6(49):152–58,
         6(50):161–68, 6(51):177–85, 6(52):193–200.

Veniaminov, Ioann
 1840   Zapiski ob ostrovakh Unalashkinskogo otdela
         (Notes on the Islands of the Unalaska District). 3
         vols. in 2. St. Petersburg: Russian American
         Company.

Virsaladze, Elena B.
 1973   The Masters of the Animals, Woods, and Waters in
         Caucasian Folklore. Paper presented at the Ninth
         International Congress of Anthropological and Eth-
         nological Sciences, Chicago, September 1–8, 1973.

Walgrave, Jan H.
 1972   Unfolding Revelation: The Nature of Doctrinal De-
         velopment. Philadelphia: Westminster Press.

West, Phoebe
 1938   An Education Program for an Aleut Village. M.A.
         thesis, University of Washington, Seattle.

Wheaton, Helen
 1945   Prekaska's Wife. New York: Dodd, Mead.

Yesner, David R.
 1977   Resource Diversity and Population Stability among
         Hunter-Gatherers. Western Canadian Journal of
         Anthropology 7(2):18–59.

Zerries, Otto
 1954   Wild und Buschgeister in Suedamerika. Wiesbaden:
         Franz Steiner.

CHAPTER SEVEN

WHY THE SOUTHEASTERN INDIANS SLAUGHTERED DEER

CHARLES M. HUDSON, JR.

THE AMERICAN INDIAN as child of nature, that softly focused image cast upon the present by the French Enlightenment, exists today only in the minds of the uninformed lay public. A smaller, more knowledgeable public is aware that many Indians—perhaps most—did conceive of themselves as existing in a special spiritual relationship with creatures, with a kind of give-and-take governing that relationship. But people who possess this knowledge about the belief system of the Indians have been troubled by what seems to be a gross contradiction: If the Indian believed that he existed in a special spiritual relationship with all other creatures, why, then, did he get into the business of killing animals, multitudes of animals, for their skins and furs, and hunt some animals almost to extinction?

There are at least three ways to explain this contradiction. First, it is possible that the Indians, because of some peculiarity of their belief system, differed radically from ourselves, so that where we so clearly see a contradiction, they saw none. Second, a closer examination of the Indian point of view might reveal features of their belief system which dissolve the contradiction—i.e., their behavior may prove to have been wholly consistent when seen in the full context of their belief system. Third, even though they may have conceived of themselves as existing in a special—even respectful—relationship with animals, the brute forces of politics and economics may have forced them to kill the animals in order to survive.

The first of these solutions to the contradiction would follow from the theory developed by Lucien Lévy-Bruhl (1966), who argued that preliterate people possess a distinctive kind of mentality, one of whose features is an indifference to contradiction.

157

Preliterate people simply do not see the contradictions we see, or if they do, they are indifferent to them. Although Lévy-Bruhl has been unfairly criticized, often for things he never wrote (Evans-Pritchard 1965:78–99), hardly anyone today seriously believes that such a vast gulf exists between the preliterate mind and our own.

The second of these solutions is argued by Calvin Martin in his book *Keepers of the Game: Indian-Animal Relationships and the Fur Trade*. From the standpoint of contextualism and cultural relativism, he argues that the contradiction clears up when we fully grasp the Indian point of view. The Indian belief system, says Martin, postulated a kind of pact between people and animals, such that if people killed game animals in moderation, and with proper precautions, then all was well, but if they did not, the animals were offended and struck back by afflicting people with diseases. Here, says Martin, is the key to dissolving the contradiction: When the Indians began suffering from European epidemic diseases, it must have seemed to them that the animals were afflicting them unfairly, thus violating their "pact," and so it was that the Indians decided to wage a kind of war on the animals, killing them without restraint. Furthermore, with their priests and medicine men unable to cure these diseases, the Indians turned readily to Christianity, which offered them an alternative belief system. Many historians have been persuaded by Martin's argument, as evidenced by the American Historical Association's having awarded his book the Beveridge Prize for 1979.

If Martin's theory is valid, then it ought to withstand testing. In the pages which follow, I test his theory against evidence from the southeastern United States. Martin developed his theory to account for the Indian hunter-gatherers of the northeastern United States, and he says that his theory should not "automatically and indiscriminately" be applied to Indians elsewhere. He says that horticulturalists, such as the Indians of the southeastern United States, probably responded to the fur trade differently from hunter-gatherers, but he nevertheless insists that his theory does apply to the horticulturalists, though perhaps less compellingly (pp. 7–8, 185). I shall argue that evidence from the Southeast does not sustain Martin's version of the Indian belief system, and moreover, that even if it did, this would not explain why the Southeastern Indians killed such large numbers of deer for their skins. I believe that the Southeastern Indians behaved as they did for economic and political reasons.

In order for Martin's theory to be applied at all in the Southeast, two conditions must first be met. First, in their belief system the Southeastern Indians should have postulated a spiritual relationship between men and animals, and they should have possessed many rules and prohibitions (taboos) which restrained their behavior with respect to animals. They should have believed that when they transgressed these rules and prohibitions, the animal spirits would retaliate by afflicting them with diseases. And second, they should have experienced great loss of life from European epidemic diseases. If these two conditions were present, Martin's theory would predict (1) that the Southeastern Indians would have blamed the animals for acting irresponsibly and maliciously in causing such terrible loss of life; (2) that after a trade in animal furs and skins began in earnest, the Southeastern Indians in their anger at the animals would have cast all rules and taboos aside and hunted their main prey animals to the point where they became scarce; and (3) that with their native healers unable to cure the epidemic diseases, the Indians would have abandoned their belief system in favor of Christianity, which would have had the added benefit of providing them with a rationale for exploiting nature without limit.

Let us examine these various propositions one by one. First, the Southeastern Indians did resemble the Northeastern Indians in postulating an important spiritual relationship between man and animal. They believed that if men killed animals carelessly, or disrespectfully, or wantonly, then the animals would strike back by afflicting them with diseases. The Cherokee theory of medicine and illness was buttressed by a mythological charter which held that diseases were caused by the enmity between men and animals, while medicines were made possible through the friendship between men and plants (Mooney 1900: 250–52). Just as the Northeastern Indians regarded their most important trade animal, the beaver, as an important disease-causing agent, so the Cherokees regarded the deer, their most important trade animal, as an important disease-causing agent.

But the Southeastern Indians also believed that disease was caused by several other factors. One could fall ill as a consequence of the actions of a sorcerer or witch in one's community (Fogelson 1975:113–31). One could fall ill through breaking rules and prohibitions governing ritually correct behavior (Mooney and Olbrechts 1932). More importantly, one could fall ill as a consequence of breaking certain moral or ritual rules, thereby offending spiritual beings higher up in the spiritual pantheon than mere animal spirits. I refer here to such beings as the Sun, or Thunder (ibid.:20–21, 24).[1]

Like all the other native people in the New World, the Southeastern Indians were devastated by epidemic diseases. Precisely when this first occurred in various parts of the Southeast can perhaps never be known with certainty. It is clear that when Hernando de Soto entered the South Carolina back country in 1540, the chiefdom of Cofitachequi had been struck by an epidemic two years earlier (Fidalgo of Elvas 1922:66). And judging from the lack of armed resistance and the scarcity of food as the de Soto expedition moved northward and westward through the mountains, it is possible that this area too may already have been struck by the epidemic (ibid.:69–72). But the populous and spirited people de Soto encountered in Coosa, in or near northeastern Alabama, and from there westward to the Mississippi River were unlikely to have yet been touched by the diseases.

Twenty years later, in 1559–61, the de Luna expedition found evidence of depopulation in the chiefdom of Coosa, though it is not clear which towns in Coosa they reached (Priestly 1928). In 1566–67 Juan Pardo heard reports of numerous aggressive warriors in the northern towns of Coosa, though he turned back before encountering them (Bandera 1569). Hence the evidence for epidemic diseases in the interior of the Southeast at this early date is not clear.[2]

Reports of epidemic diseases among the Southeastern Indians became more definite with the founding of the Spanish missions in Florida and eastern Georgia in the late sixteenth and early seventeenth centuries. In 1655, for example, a series of smallpox epidemics struck in Florida. The population of the province of Apalachee is reported to have declined from 16,000 in 1638 to 5,000 in 1676 (Matter 1972:131).

It is evident that the two conditions for applying Martin's theory are present. Let us see how the theory fares.

First of all, did the Southeastern Indians blame animals for the epidemics? This is no easy question. Even harder to come by than dates and accurate statistics for the epidemics is historical evidence about how the Indians explained their causes. To my knowledge, the best instance of such explanation in the Southeast is reported by James Adair in his *History of the American Indians*. Smallpox broke out among the Cherokees in 1738. The reason the epidemic occurred, an old priest told Adair, was that it was punishment for the sexual promiscuity of their young people. In particular, they had committed their heinous acts in the sacred corn and bean fields of the priests, which lay close by the mounds on which the town houses were built, where dances and other social affairs were held (Adair 1775:232).

This explanation is not what Martin's theory would predict. But it is, as we shall see later, consistent with certain theoretical notions which modern social anthropologists have developed in their study of preliterate belief systems. Indeed, I cannot find that Martin cites a single piece of evidence of Indian reasoning that a particular epidemic was caused by animal spirits. Instead, given the assumptions and beliefs of the Northeastern Indians, Martin argues that it is *reasonable* that the Indians would have concluded that the epidemics were caused by an inexplicably vicious attack by animal spirits.

Martin, however, is overlooking a structural pattern that is typical of preliterate belief systems—namely, that spiritual beings exist in a hierarchy (Horton 1967; Skorupski 1976:205–23). The spiritual beings at the lower levels of the hierarchy are the ones used to explain the everyday problems of life which consume most people's time. They explain, for example, the most frequent kinds of minor illnesses. In contrast, the spiritual beings at the highest level of the hierarchy, though remote from everyday life, hold sway over all else. Given this structural pattern, it would make sense that any sweeping or unprecedented epidemic disease would be explained in terms of having been caused by higher deities. The account the old Cherokee priest gave James Adair appears to be consistent with this pattern. That is, Cherokee young people committed such grievous moral violations that an extraordinary punishment was inflicted on the Cherokees, presumably by the more remote spirits in the Cherokee pantheon.

It is doubtful, then, that the Southeastern Indians did blame animals for the epidemics. But if we leave that aside and go on, we still find ample evidence that the Southeastern Indians hunted for trade to the point where their prey became scarce.

Unlike the Indian trade in the Northeast, which was primarily a trade in furs, the Indian trade in the Southeast was primarily a trade in deerskins, and in the early days it was a trade in captured Indian slaves, with furs clearly of secondary importance. This trade reached the Southeastern Indians from Virginia, first through Indian middlemen perhaps as early as the 1650s, and later through traders employed by Abraham Wood and William Byrd I (Franklin 1932). But the trade with the Southeastern Indians did not begin in earnest until the founding of Charles Town in 1670. Here, the trade began almost casually, as a plantation trade. At first the planters would hire Indians to hunt for them, to bring in a supply of game and deerskins. But as time went on, other Indians came in to the plantations to trade. Between 1680 and 1690 traders from Carolina were going into the interior to trade for Indian slaves and deerskins (Crane 1929:21). Deerskins were the first commodity

Carolina produced, and the slaughter of Virginia deer was tremendous. Hundreds of thousands of deerskins were exported from Charles Town in the early eighteenth century (Crane 1928:111–12). It is difficult to determine just when deer became scarce because the population of the Indians was declining along with the deer. But by the late eighteenth century, certainly, deer were scarce in parts of the Southeast (Hawkins 1916:72; Mad Dog 1935).

Moreover, in the interest of commerce the Southeastern Indians hunted other Indians with the same ferocity with which they hunted deer and beaver. By 1690, within twenty years of the founding of Charles Town, the English had destroyed the Spanish mission system in Guale, in what is now coastal Georgia. In 1704, Colonel James Moore led 50 whites and 1,000 Indian mercenaries into the Apalachee missions of western Florida. Within a few months they completely destroyed a mission system that had taken the Spanish friars a hundred years to build. Moore claims that he and his men took away as slaves 325 men and 4,000 women and children. Many mission Indians were killed in battle, and Moore's mercenaries later tortured others to death. Moore lost 4 whites and 15 Indians (Matter 1972:294). Two decades later, the Apalachee Indians were nearer to extinction than were beaver or deer.

Looking at the third implication of Martin's theory in the Southeast, we see that these Indians, like those of the Northeast, gradually abandoned their aboriginal belief system and embraced Christianity, though not in the same way as in the Northeast. Certainly there is no evidence that the Southeastern Indians abruptly saw the futility of their native priests and healers and embraced Christianity as a consequence. The Spanish built the first missions in the Southeast, but no one can say that the Indians flocked to them. In fact, historians have been at pains to explain why it took so long for the Spanish to succeed in missionizing Florida (Matter 1972).

In 1549, a ship carrying the first missionary to the Southeast, Luis Cáncer de Barbastro, dropped anchor apparently near present-day Tampa Bay. But the Indians captured and killed two of Cáncer's fellow priests, and when he went ashore to see about them, the Indians killed Cáncer too (Quinn 1977:228–30). Next, the Jesuits, in their very first mission attempt in the New World, tried to convert the Florida Indians. After failing, all the Jesuits were removed in 1572. The first truly successful missions in Florida were established by the Franciscans, beginning in 1573. But even they suffered from a series of violent Indian uprisings in which many of the friars were killed. In 1655 the Franciscans claimed to have converted 26,000 Indians, though this is almost certainly an exaggeration (Matter 1972:107). Moreover, the depth of these conversions may be doubted. The very next year, in 1656, a great Indian rebellion began in Timucua and spread to Apalachee. More significantly, there is evidence that some of the Indian mercenaries who accompanied Colonel James Moore were apostates from the missions. They would almost certainly have been the ones who supplied Moore with the intelligence with which to plan and execute his raids.

British attempts at missionizing the Indians were mostly afterthoughts to their commercial interests. In Virginia in the early days of the colony, the British attempted to *educate* the Indians by having Indian boys attend schools and colleges. But this failed because when the boys returned to their people they necessarily reverted back to their native culture. William Byrd advocated intermarriage between poor whites and Indians as a way of converting the heathen, but English colonists never showed much enthusiasm for his plan (Robinson 1952:152–68).

The mission effort of the Society for the Propagation of the Gospel (S.P.G.) in South Carolina was unimpressive. Thomas Nairne, the first Indian agent for South Carolina, observed in 1705 that many of the Indians who had been enslaved by the Carolinians had already been converted to Christianity by the Spanish, but because the Carolinians gave them no religious instruction they were reverting back to their old ways. To correct this, Francis Le Jau, the first S.P.G. missionary in Carolina, arrived in 1706. Le Jau had evidently learned about the conditions of the Indians by interrogating white traders. He set aside one day a week to give instruction to the Indian and Negro slaves in his parish. He advocated that some English boys be sent to live among the Indians to learn their languages, but apparently none were sent. Seventeen years later, in 1723, Francis Varnod, another S.P.G. missionary in Carolina, was idly advocating the same plan (Pennington 1935; Klingberg 1939).

Even the Methodists failed. Charles and John Wesley's Methodism fell on deaf Indian ears in Savannah in the 1730s (Wesley 1906). The Southeastern Indians did not begin to turn seriously to American culture and Christianity until the beginning of the nineteenth century. And even then they did not simply cast aside their own belief systems. The Upper Creeks were capable of drawing upon native ideology to organize a potent "nativistic" movement in the early years of the nineteenth century. In fact, James Mooney found native healers very much at work among the Cherokees in the late nineteenth century. They had retained a surprising amount of their traditional knowledge, and some of them had even written it down in little books using the Sequoyan syllabary (Mooney and Olbrechts 1932).

Here we can pause and calculate the extent to which Martin's theory applies to the Southeastern Indians. From the meager evidence that is available, he appears to be wrong in his contention that the Indians would have blamed animal spirits for their having been stricken by European epidemics. He is correct in predicting that the Indians hunted with great ferocity anything the traders selected as desirable—deer, beaver, and human beings—but he is not necessarily correct in saying why. He is correct in saying that the Southeastern Indians would in time give up their own belief system in favor of American culture and Christianity, but they do not seem to have done so in the way his theory specifies. The road to Christianity in the aboriginal Southeast was both rocky and circuitous.

It is clear that Martin's theory does not fare well in the Southeast. But the problem is not that he has insufficient understanding of the Southeastern Indian belief system. For even if one understood perfectly every part of the Indian belief system, it still would not provide an adequate explanation for why the Indians slaughtered game animals after European contact. With European colonization, and particularly with English colonization, the Indians became involved in a new economic and political order. This new order required them to undergo a social and economic transformation so fundamental that what they believed or valued bore little relationship to what they had to do to survive.

If we are to understand why the Southeastern Indians slaughtered deer, we cannot ignore the fact that much of what the Indians did after European contact was shaped by economic and political imperatives, imperatives that are perhaps clearer in the Southeast than in the Northeast. When the first English colonists landed in 1670 on the Carolina coast, they found the Cusabo and Cusso Indians thereabouts in mortal fear of some Indians who had recently appeared from the interior and had begun raiding them. They called these Indians "Westoes." The Westoes had guns, and they were said to be cannibals, perhaps because they took people prisoner, and these people were never seen again. No one can be quite sure who these Westoes were. Several theories have been put forth about their linguistic and cultural identity. But no matter what language they spoke, or what culture they possessed, their position in the larger Southeastern scheme of things is clear. They were Indian slavers, armed by the Virginians, who were capturing Southern Indians and taking them north to the slave market in Virginia (Crane 1929:6–12; Snell 1972:7–19).

When the French reached the lower Mississippi River and Gulf Coast in 1699, they found that the Indians there were utterly terrified. They had recently been raided by Chickasaws from the interior who were armed with guns supplied by Carolina traders. These Chickasaws had captured some of the Indians whom the French had encountered. The captives were no doubt sold on the slave market in Charles Town (Crane 1929:67).

The lesson is clear. Wherever the English established plantations in the seventeenth century, the Indians in the vicinity had the choice of buying guns to defend themselves, or else of being killed or enslaved. The Cusabos and Cussos, for example, began trading deerskins for guns immediately after the founding of Charles Town (Snell 1972:8–9). The bow and arrow was no match for the English musket. Anyone who doubts this should examine Colonel James Moore's raids into Apalachee in 1704. The Apalachees, who could have had no more than a handful of Spanish guns, were killed and enslaved almost to a man. The Apalachee Indians are now extinct.

We are nearer now to an answer to our basic question. The Southeastern Indians slaughtered deer (and were prompted to enslave and kill each other) because of their position on the outer fringes of an expanding modern world-system. As Immanuel Wallerstein (1974) has shown, this world-system first took shape in Europe in the late fifteenth and early sixteenth centuries. It was unlike any political and economic system that had existed before it. It resembled an empire, but it was not an empire. In fact, the colonial Southeast is a good place in which to discern some of the differences between the modern world-system and an empire because it was here that the English, who would eventually dominate the world-system, came into collision with the Spanish, who were attempting to build an empire.

In an empire the rulers attempt to exercise political control over all of the people within it. Spain, for example, attempted to annex parts of the New World, including Florida, into her empire, with its massive and expensive bureaucracy. Like other empires before, Spain extracted *tribute* from her outlying colonies. Since Florida had neither wealth that could easily be extracted, nor a large and easily controlled labor force, Spain established the weakest sort of tribute extraction—a mission system. The mission Indians produced food for the friars, and some food for the officials and the military centered in St. Augustine, while producing yet a little more for illegal trade. And all the while, the Franciscans were attempting to transform the Indians into obedient Spaniards, teaching them to speak Spanish and perform Catholic rituals.

In contrast, in the modern world-system there is a core region which establishes *economic* relations with its colonial periphery. The English who landed on the Carolina coast never seriously tried to make the Indians into Englishmen. As we have seen, the English missionary effort was little more than a pallid afterthought. If the Indians could not produce commodities, they were on the road to cultural extinction. In fact, the Indians around the English colonies would eventually be extinct anyway. What England wanted from her American colonies were various agricultural and forest products: cattle, rice, indigo, timber, and naval stores. All of these require land, and the Indians were sitting on some of this land. Whether they knew it or not, the best that the Indians could hope for was survival in the short term. This was especially true of those Indians who were located nearest to the English frontier.

In 1671, the year after Charles Town was founded, the Cussos became angry when English cattle got into their cornfields. When armed conflict broke out, the Carolinians captured some of the Cussos and sold them into slavery in the West Indies. In 1674 the same fate befell the Stono Indians, whose towns and fields were close to the colonial settlements (Snell 1972:12–13).

Given the nature of the English system, the only way the Indians could prolong their survival was to produce commodities—deerskins and Indian slaves—which they could trade for guns and other necessities. Earlier I mentioned the Virginia traders who employed the Westoes as slavers and as middlemen. In 1674 Henry Woodward of Carolina undercut the Virginia traders by making a deal with the Westoes. The terms of the deal were that the Westoes would raid the interior for slaves in exchange for a monopoly on trade goods from Carolina (Snell 1972:19–20).

Hence, the initial strategy of proprietary South Carolina was to establish good relations with a group of Indians just beyond the range of the cattle herders, and these Indians would then enslave and exploit other Indians in the interior. But there were no guarantees in this dangerous game. The proprietors, who tried to run the Carolina colony from England, favored the

Westoes, but a powerful faction within the Carolina colony wanted to profit from this trade themselves. In 1680 this faction teamed up with the "Savannahs" (Upper Creeks from Apalachee), and together they attacked the Westoes. When the shooting was over, only about fifty Westoes remained. The others had been killed or enslaved (Snell 1972:25–27, 34).[3] Then, for about ten years, the Savannahs served as mercenaries and slave catchers for the Carolinians.

To maximize his chances for survival, an eighteenth-century Southeastern Indian had to do several things. He had to live in the interior, out of range of European cattle, forestry, and agriculture. In the early days he had to produce a commodity which was valuable enough to earn him some protection from English slavers. Later, the Indian slave trade subsided, but at the same time that this occurred, the political rivalry between various colonial powers heated up. The Indians attempted to use this rivalry to their own advantage. In exchange for European trade goods, the Indians would promise political alignment, though these promises were never as firm nor as binding as the Europeans wished. And it was not altogether a good arrangement for the Indians because they were sometimes killed when the rivalry heated up and they *had* to take sides.

Paradoxically, in this setting the only good fortune a Southeastern Indian could hope for was to have around him the greatest possible number of European interests contending for supremacy in the world-system.[4] As the contenders in the Southeastern arena eliminated each other one by one, the fate of the Southeastern Indians was progressively determined. After having been pressed for over a century in a one-on-one situation with the Spaniards, soon after the founding of Charles Town the Lower Creeks moved from the Chattahoochee River northeastward to the Ocmulgee River in order to be located between the English and the Spanish. Many of them served as English mercenaries in the raids on the Spanish missions in Guale, Apalachee, and Timucua. But after the Spanish mission system was effectively destroyed by Moore's raid, the position of the

Lower Creeks on the Ocmulgee River was seriously weakened. It was them against the English, one-on-one again. They began to suffer at the hands of the traders, who mistreated them badly. The Yamassee War of 1715 was a direct outcome of this mistreatment, and when it was over, the Lower Creeks withdrew back to the Chattahoochee.

As the eighteenth century wore on, one after another the world-system contenders in the Southeast fell away. With the French eliminated at the close of the Seven Years' War, the position of all the Southeastern Indians was weakened. When the British were eliminated at the close of the American Revolution, there were only two contenders left in the Southeast: Indian and American, one-on-one. In fact, at this point the conflict became racial in character, with Indian versus white. "Removal" was just around the corner.

My contention is that these are the terms in which we are to properly understand why the Southeastern Indians slaughtered deer. It is not that there were no other factors intervening in specific times and places. What I am prepared to argue, however, is that it never made much difference what the Indians believed about the proper relationship of man to nature. Quite simply, when the bases of their survival changed, they did what they had to do in order to survive.[5]

This leads us to a fundamental question raised by Calvin Martin's book, the question that presumably aroused his interest in the first place. Namely, what relationship exists between human beliefs and values on the one hand, and human behavior on the other? To what degree do men behave consistently with what they believe?

It is an issue that is more difficult to resolve than any of the others we have considered. It is a problem about which philosophers have argued interminably. Anthropologists who have done intensive fieldwork in preliterate societies have often noted that what people believe to be the case in their society, and what they believe ought to be the case, and what they actually do, seldom coincide in any simple way (Beattie 1964:

34–38). And social anthropologists, because of their field work, are probably less likely than historians to be misled by ideal culture patterns which are apt to show up in documentary evidence. This point has been made by the anthropologist E. E. Evans-Pritchard, who asks how "an Oxford don [can] work himself into the mind of a serf of Louis the Pious" (1962:58). The historian Keith Thomas has made a similar observation (1963). Both Evans-Pritchard and Thomas argue for a closer rapprochement between anthropology and history on the grounds that each can profit from the strengths of the other.

Marx maintained that men's belief systems arise out of their modes of production. If this is so, then one would expect some sort of consistency between what men believe and what men do, a consistency that we have found missing among the Southeastern and Northeastern Indians. But in times of profound economic transformation such consistency would not be expected, especially when a radically new economic order is in the making. In such a case, people might very well hold beliefs and values from an older order while having to behave and act in accordance with a newly emerging order. Even though the Southeastern Indians might have felt bad about slaughtering the deer, they slaughtered them anyway. Perhaps they were like the Walrus in *Through the Looking Glass*, who wept for the dear little oysters, but ate them every one.

My fundamental concern here has been the Indians of the southeastern United States, but I suspect that my argument applies to the Indians of the Northeast as well. Martin himself mentions that several northern groups were almost completely wiped out by Iroquois who were armed with English guns (pp. 52, 101). And he mentions that in the middle of the seventeenth century, the Frenchman Denys observed that some trade goods had become "indispensable necessities" to the Indians (p. 61). These were very strong inducements to trade.

In *Keepers of the Game* Calvin Martin has done what anthropologists have long advocated. He has attempted to grasp the "Indian point of view" and to make this point of view intrinsic in the piece of Indian history he has written. Why then has there been so much to criticize? Partly it is because taking the Indian point of view requires one to analyze and render intelligible the belief system by means of which the Indians in question constructed reality. More often than not, in regard to Indians in the past, such an analysis is difficult or impossible because of faulty or nonexistent evidence. The only sure way to "factor out" the beliefs and assumptions that Indians of earlier days lived by is to analyze native texts, and such texts are sometimes lacking, or when they are available they are often heavily Europeanized. Moreover, even when authentic texts are available, reading them correctly requires some theoretical sophistication. Some of the very first questions addressed by anthropologists concerned the nature of the mentality and religious beliefs of preliterate people. The attempt to answer these questions has produced a voluminous literature that now goes back over a hundred years.

Martin's use of the "Indian point of view," however, can be faulted on more fundamental grounds. It is simply this: While it is true that ethnohistorians ought to exhaust every means of taking the Indian point of view into account, there is, nonetheless, a limit to what the Indian point of view can explain. After Spain, France, and England had established viable colonies in North America, the Indian point of view can bring little to bear, for example, on questions pertaining to the kinds of conflicts that occurred among these colonial powers, or to the various means they used to form alliances with Indians, or to the long-term implications of these alliances for the Indians. The answers to most of these questions can be found only in the political and economic forces that shaped colonial history, and particularly those forces that were produced by the early evolution of the modern world-system.

Notes

Part of the research on which this paper is based was done in 1977–78, while I held a fellowship in the Center for the History of the American Indian, Newberry Library. I am grateful to Stephen Kowalewski for helpful comments on an earlier version.

1. In places it is clear that Martin recognizes that the Northeastern Indians also acknowledged disease-causing agents other than animal spirits, but he consistently assigns these to a subsidiary role (see, e.g., p. 54n).
2. I am grateful to Chester DePratter for pointing out this apparent discrepancy between the Pardo and Luna expeditions into Coosa.
3. These enslaved Westoes were diverse in their ethnic origins—Appamattox, Cherokees, Chatot, "Yanorks," and Winyahs—suggesting that the Westoes may have consisted of a melange of different peoples.
4. Emperor Brims of the Lower Creeks perhaps understood this better than any contemporary Southeastern Indian leader.
5. In this light, the formalist-substantivist controversy begs the question. What is at issue is not so much the nature of the aboriginal Indian economic systems as it is the nature of the world-system that transformed them. Cf. Martin 1978:10–15.

References Cited

Adair, James
    1775   The History of the American Indians. London.

Bandera, Juan de la
    1569   Proceedings of the Account which Captain Juan Pardo gave of the Entry which he made into the Land of the Floridas. Translation in the North Carolina State Archives, Raleigh.

Beattie, John
    1964   Other Cultures. New York: Free Press.

Crane, Verner W.
    1928   The Southern Frontier, 1670–1732. Durham: Duke University Press.

Evans-Pritchard, E. E.
    1962   Essays in Social Anthropology. London: Faber and Faber.
    1965   Theories of Primitive Religion. Oxford: Clarendon Press.

Fidalgo of Elvas
    1922   Discovery of Florida: The True Relation by a Fidalgo of Elvas. *In* Narratives of the Career of Hernando de Soto, Vol. 1. Edward Gaylord Bourne, ed. New York: Allerton.

Fogelson, Raymond
    1975   An Analysis of Cherokee Sorcery and Witchcraft. *In* Four Centuries of Southern Indians, ed. Charles Hudson, pp. 113–31. Athens: University of Georgia Press.

Franklin, W. Neil
    1932   Virginia and the Cherokee Indian Trade, 1673–1754. The East Tennessee Historical Society's Publications 4:3–21.

Hawkins, Benjamin
1916   Letters of Benjamin Hawkins. Georgia Historical Society Collections, Vol. 9.
Horton, Robin
1967   African Traditional Thought and Western Science. Africa 37:50–71, 155–87.
Klingberg, Frank J.
1939   The Indian Frontier in South Carolina as Seen by the S.P.G. Missionary. Journal of Southern History 5:479–500.
Lévy-Bruhl, Lucien
1966   How Natives Think. Lilian A. Clare, trans. New York: Washington Square Press.
Mad Dog
1935   Talk from the Indian Chief Mad Dog, May 31, 1801. Florida Historical Quarterly 13:165–66.
Martin, Calvin
1978   Keepers of the Game: Indian-Animal Relationships and the Fur Trade. Berkeley: University of California Press.
Matter, Robert A.
1972   The Spanish Missions of Florida: The Friars versus the Governors in the "Golden Age," 1606–1690. Ph.D. dissertation, University of Washington.
Mooney, James
1900   Myths of the Cherokee. Nineteenth Annual Report of the Bureau of American Ethnology. Washington, D.C.
Mooney, James, and Frans M. Olbrechts
1932   The Swimmer Manuscript. Bureau of American Ethnology Bulletin, No. 99. Washington, D.C.
Pennington, Edgar Legare
1935   The Reverend Francis Le Jau's Work among the Indians and Negro Slaves. Journal of Southern History 1:442–58.

Priestly, Herbert I., ed. and trans.
  1928   The Luna Papers: Documents Relating to the Expedition of Don Tristan de Luna y Arellano for the Conquest of La Florida in 1559–1561. 2 vols. De Land, Florida.
Quinn, David
  1977   North America from Earliest Discovery to First Settlements: The Norse Voyages to 1612. New York: Harper & Row.
Robinson, W. Stitt, Jr.
  1952   Indian Education and Missions in Colonial Virginia. Journal of Southern History 18:152–68.
Shorupski, John
  1976   Symbol and Theory. Cambridge: Cambridge University Press.
Snell, William Robert
  1972   Indian Slavery in Colonial South Carolina, 1671–1795. Ph.D. dissertation, University of Alabama.
Thomas, Keith
  1963   History and Anthropology. Past and Present 24:3–24.
Wallerstein, Immanuel
  1974   The Modern World-System: Capitalist Agriculture and the Origins of the European World Economy in the Sixteenth Century. New York: Academic Press.
Wesley, John
  1906   The Journal of the Rev. John Wesley. New York: Dutton.

CHAPTER EIGHT

ANIMALS AND DISEASE
IN INDIAN BELIEF

WILLIAM C. STURTEVANT

PART OF Calvin Martin's thesis holds that much previous work on his topic has been flawed by the ethnocentric assumption that Indian motives were those of Western economic man (Martin 1978:10–15). In this I suspect he is right. But he goes on to suggest that in fact what was operating was a quite different Indian philosophy and world view, which held that there was an agreement, a sort of treaty, involving reciprocal obligations and duties between humans and animals, in which animals offered themselves to be killed and aided humans in difficulties such as illness, provided that humans kept up their side of the bargain in continuing to treat animals properly, not inflicting needless suffering upon them, not killing more than they needed, and treating the bodies of those they killed with proper respect. Martin then suggests that when massive epidemics struck the Indians, these were interpreted as the animals' defaulting on their side of the bargain and that in response humans retaliated by an uncontrolled slaughter of animals—especially those now important for the fur trade—as a sort of revenge.

When I first heard this part of his thesis, my reaction was that Martin's interpretation of Indian beliefs and attitudes was unlikely, and in fact itself involved an ethnocentric interpretation of the historical and ethnographic data. This opinion derived from my fieldwork on Florida Seminole medical beliefs and practices (Sturtevant 1954), and to a lesser degree from my briefer work with modern Iroquois on largely different topics (Sturtevant 1952–65). In Southern Indian belief, specific diseases are both caused and cured by specific animal species. From this Southern point of view, I doubted that in Indian belief humans in general had an agreement with animals in general,

179

and especially that new diseases could be blamed on animals in general or on any species at random, and revenge would then be taken on specific species which had not been shown to be, in native belief, the causes—and the curers—of the new diseases.

But in examining the ethnographic literature on Northern Indian concepts of disease and its cure (a literature that is surprisingly skimpy), I failed to find even a native theory that specific species of animals cause specific diseases. Martin himself presents no evidence that this was the case. He writes: "Because shamans lost their ability to cure diseases—diseases that were *probably* originally assigned to offended wildlife—the Indian lost faith in the traditional avenues of spiritual redress. Man thus became hostile toward an animal kingdom which he was convinced had broken faith with him" (p. 148; my emphasis). "Probably" is a careful historian's signal that he is about to go beyond his documentary evidence. Similarly, notice the import of "seemingly" in the following: "Is it not reasonable to assume that these people, who were *seemingly* accustomed to blaming offended wildlife for their sicknesses, would have blamed them as well for the new contagions? . . . In an attempt to extricate himself from their morbid grip, the Indian sought to destroy his wildlife tormentors: he went on a war of revenge, a war which soon became transformed into the historic fur trade" (p. 146; my emphasis).

There appears to be no evidence that Northern Indians blamed wildlife in this way; rather, they blamed themselves for contravening the rules governing the relations between humans and animals. But even if they did blame animals, Martin must show, as he has not, that there was believed to be an association between specific new diseases (of European origin) and specific animal species, and that the "revenge" was taken on *those* species. It seems contrary to Indian logic to hold that if one animal species fails us, we may then take revenge on another animal species, or on all animals. That is European logic, making a sharp, non-Indian dichotomy between humans and animals, and overequating animals of different kinds.

Lévi-Strauss has analyzed our peculiar traditional European notions of the relations of humans with animals, explaining that the analytical concept of totemism represents "the projection outside our own universe, as though by a kind of exorcism, of mental attitudes incompatible with the exigency of a discontinuity between man and nature which Christian thought has held to be essential" (1963:3). The idea of a continuity between man and nature is so un-Christian as to require a special label, totemism, as though it were a sort of psychopathic condition.[1] Martin's suggested Northern Indian conception of the relations between humans and wildlife falls outside Lévi-Strauss's analysis of the possible relations between culture and nature, between humans and animals. He posits a relation between all humans (or all members of a society) and all animals, whereas Lévi-Strauss sees, in accord with the ethnographic data, the possibilities as permutations of relations between, on the cultural or social side, groups (such as clans) or individual humans and, on the natural or animal side, categories (such as species) or particular individual animals (Lévi-Strauss 1963:16–17).

However, among the most difficult parts of an alien culture to comprehend are world view, the concept of humans and animals, the nature of persons, the ideas of causation, and the theory of disease. And once comprehended, they are very difficult to explain. In a volume largely devoted to the mental life of the Naskapi, Frank G. Speck, perhaps the most gifted and experienced ethnographer of Eastern Indians, commented that "to arrive at a definite idea of how the manifestations of nature are pictured in the native mind is one of the most difficult of matters" (Speck 1935a:55). A. I. Hallowell, whose Ojibwa fieldwork was extended, intensive, and informed by a sophisticated psychological and philosophical background, frankly admitted the great difficulty he had both in coming to an understanding of the Ojibwa view of these matters, and in explaining the understanding he had reached (e.g., Hallowell 1954:79–80; 1960:358–59, 362–64; 1963:399–400). Preston (1975) is convincing on the same issue.

World view and the relation of man to nature are perhaps the most difficult and problematical aspects of ethnohistorical reconstruction, comparable to or even greater in difficulty than the reconstruction of the individual personalities and motives of members of bygone and alien societies. Here particularly, one cannot trust older contemporary sources, even those by the best-informed and most sympathetic observers. Where modern ethnography largely fails, we cannot expect seventeenth- or eighteenth- or nineteenth-century authors to do even as well. While I have examined a number of different modern sources on Northern Indians—Speck on the Naskapi (1935*a*) and Penobscot (1935*b*); Tanner (1979), Preston (1975), and Rogers (1973) on the Cree; Jenness (1935) and Landes (1968) on the Ojibwa; and Ridington (1971) on the Beaver Indians—I prefer to cite only Hallowell on the Ojibwa, as the best ethnographer who has devoted intensive time and thought to these matters (and one whom Martin often cites, although I think he misunderstands him). The others, fine ethnographers all, were less interested in these topics. Even so, if one reads them in the light of Hallowell's analysis, all their reports are consistent, with variations expectable for different societies in the same general culture area. None provides evidence supporting this aspect of Martin's hypothesis.

According to Hallowell (1963:402), "the Ojibwa do not entertain any concept of a natural world, comparable to that which has become characteristic of the view of modern Western culture." "The concept of 'supernatural' presupposes a concept of the 'natural.' The latter is not present in Ojibwa thought" (1960:366).

"In the Ojibwa universe, events may be said to be the consequence of the behavior of persons. The most ready explanation of events is a 'personalistic' theory of causation. *Who* did it? or *Who* is responsible? is always the crucial question" (Hallowell 1963:403). But "persons" in this and other passages of Hallowell's writings on the Ojibwa labels a particular and non-European concept: "persons" are not just human beings. Humans—that is, Ojibwas—are only one class of persons. The others are what Hallowell calls "other-than-human beings." Humans and these other-than-humans share the characteristic of potential metamorphosis from one into another kind of person; this is a distinctive characteristic of persons, but not of all animate beings. Not all game animals, for example, are persons, but only the "owners" or "masters" of the various species of plants and animals. "Other-than-human" persons also include the Four Winds, the Sun and Moon, the Thunderbirds, and the characters in myths. All these are referred to as "Our Grandfathers" (ibid.:403–5). "In the behavioral world of the Ojibwa, no sharp line can be drawn between animals, *pawáganak* [i.e., dream visitors, guardian spirits], men, or the spirits of the dead on the basis of outward bodily aspect or appearance alone" (Hallowell 1954:179).

The relation between humans and game animals is an interpersonal one; but the other-than-human persons in this relation are not individual game animals but rather their "masters" or "keepers." It is they who send the animals to offer themselves to be killed by the hunter.

The general Ojibwa idea of causation was personalistic. What, then, caused disease? According to Hallowell, "any serious illness is associated with some prior conduct which involved an infraction of moral rules: the illness is explained as a penalty for bad conduct. It is a consequence of behavioral deviation from expected patterns of interpersonal relations, whether between human persons or between a human being and an other-than-human person" (Hallowell 1963:410). But there seems to be a difference between illness due to a failure in proper relations between different human persons, which is curable, and one due to a failure in proper relations between a human person and other-than-human persons, which is not curable. This is true even when the violation of one's behavioral obligations to other-than-human persons is inadvertent, such as for example an unknowing violation of a food taboo (ibid.:417).

Hallowell almost directly contradicts Martin's thesis: "'Our grandfathers' . . . do not afflict human beings with illness. . . . It is true that if men do not treat game animals properly, the 'persons' who are their 'masters' will not allow these animals to be caught. But the human offenders are not afflicted with sickness on this account." There is no "belief in the punishing roles of other-than-human persons" (Hallowell 1963:411–12). "An illness which is thought to eventuate from the violation of moral obligations to 'our grandfathers' cannot be interpreted as stemming from their anger" (ibid.:418). Martin suggests (p. 129*n*) that Hallowell "appears to contradict himself" on this matter. But the complexity and strangeness of Ojibwa belief require one to take Hallowell's whole description into account. The "retribution" for cruelty to animals, the "disease sanction" that is applicable (Hallowell 1963:419), does not imply that the "persons" who are the "masters" of the animals punish humans by "afflicting" them with disease (as Martin seems to interpret Hallowell 1963:413–14). Rather, humans become afflicted (intransitively) as a result of their own failure in interpersonal relations with the "masters," with their lack of respect to animals that offends the "masters."

According to Hallowell, then, the animals have behaved properly. If there is illness, the human must have failed somehow in interpersonal relations, not the animals. The problem is to discover what this human misbehavior may have been. The discovery, if it comes, is equivalent to a confession, and a cure should follow if there has been a breach in interhuman relations (Hallowell 1963:412–14). If a curer—a shaman, if you will—fails to cure, this may well be explained as a consequence of some past interpersonal failing *of the curer* (ibid.:421–23).[2]

In any case, it is clear that in the Ojibwa view—and this, I believe, is the only Northern Indian view of these matters of which we have any real understanding—it would make no sense whatsoever to take revenge on game animals for human illness.

Martin's book has raised very important issues about the nature of historical and anthropological explanation, about our own professional world view, including our notions of causation. The arguments it has engendered illustrate that we do not adequately understand our own scholarly world view, or at least have difficulty in articulating it. It should be much more difficult to reach agreement about the world views of other cultures.

Notes

1. For a convincing analysis of the importance and singularity (in a somewhat different connection) of Euro-American ideas about metaphorical relations between human society and the animal kingdom, see Sahlins 1976.
2. Confirmatory evidence comes from Mary B. Black, a more recent fieldworker among the Ojibwa, who has undertaken extensive explorations of semantics and cognition in domains very relevant to Martin's thesis, using techniques rather different from Hallowell's. Black 1973 discusses the subtleties of Ojibwa "questioning etiquette," leading one to deduce the probability of error by unskilled ethnographers, especially in matters so sensitive (to the Ojibwa) as concepts of misfortune and the relations of humans to nonhuman persons and animals. Black 1977b deals with the Ojibwa classification of "living things," quoting and explicating Hallowell's writings on the topic. Black 1977a helps clarify the "power-control" relations among "living things"; and Black 1976:141, 144, 146–47, on the Ojibwa distinction between (loosely) "important game animals" and "other animals," tends to contradict Martin's hypothesis equating all game animals.

References Cited

Black, Mary B.

1973   Ojibwa Questioning Etiquette and Use of Ambiguity. Studies in Linguistics 23:13–29.

1976   Semantic Variability in a Northern Ojibwa Community. Papers in Linguistics 9(3–4):129–57. Edmonton.

1977a   Ojibwa Power Belief System. *In* The Anthropology of Power: Ethnographic Studies from Asia, Oceania, and the New World, ed. R. D. Fogelson and R. N. Adams, pp. 141–51. New York: Academic Press.

1977b   Ojibwa Taxonomy and Percept Ambiguity. Ethos 5(1):90–118.

Hallowell, A. Irving

1954   The Self and Its Behavioural Environment. *In* Explorations 2:106–65. (*As reprinted in* Culture and Experience, by A. Irving Hallowell, pp. 75–110, 172–82. Philadelphia: University of Pennsylvania Press, 1955.)

1960   Ojibwa Ontology, Behavior, and World View. *In* Culture in History: Essays in Honor of Paul Radin, ed. Stanley Diamond, pp. 19–52. New York: Columbia University Press. (*As reprinted in* Contributions to Anthropology: Selected Papers of A. Irving Hallowell, ed. Raymond D. Fogelson, pp. 357–90. Chicago: University of Chicago Press, 1976.)

1963   Ojibwa World View and Disease. *In* Man's Image in Medicine and Anthropology, ed. Iago Galdston, pp. 258–315. New York: International Universities Press. (*As reprinted in* Contributions to Anthropology, pp. 391–448 [see above].)

Jenness, Diamond
  1935   The Ojibwa Indians of Parry Island: Their Social
          and Religious Life. Canada Department of Mines.
          National Museum of Canada Bulletin No. 78. An-
          thropological Series No. 17. Ottawa.
Landes, Ruth
  1968   Ojibwa Religion and the Midéwiwin. Madison: Uni-
          versity of Wisconsin Press.
Lévi-Strauss, Claude
  1963   Totemism. Trans. Rodney Needham [*from* Le toté-
          misme aujourd'hui, Paris, 1962]. Boston: Beacon
          Press.
Martin, Calvin
  1978   Keepers of the Game: Indian-Animal Relationships
          and the Fur Trade. Berkeley: University of Califor-
          nia Press.
Preston, Richard J.
  1975   Cree Narrative: Expressing the Personal Meanings
          of Events. National Museum of Man Mercury Se-
          ries. Canadian Ethnology Service Paper No. 30.
          Ottawa: National Museums of Canada.
Ridington, Robin
  1971   Beaver Dreaming and Singing. Anthropologica
          13:115–28.
Rogers, Edward S.
  1973   The Quest for Food and Furs: The Mistassini Cree,
          1953–1954. National Museum of Man, Publications
          in Ethnology No. 5. Ottawa: National Museums of
          Canada.
Sahlins, Marshall
  1976   Folk Dialectics of Nature and Culture. *In* The Use
          and Abuse of Biology: An Anthropological Critique
          of Sociobiology, by Marshall Sahlins, pp. 93–107.
          Ann Arbor: University of Michigan Press.
Speck, Frank G.
  1935a   Naskapi: The Savage Hunters of the Labrador Pen-
          insula. Norman: University of Oklahoma Press.

1935*b*   Penobscot Tales and Religious Beliefs. Journal of
        American Folklore 48(187):1–107.
Sturtevant, William C.
1954   The Mikasuki Seminole: Medical Beliefs and Prac-
        tices. Ph.D. dissertation, Yale University.
1952–65 Notes on about six months' ethnographic fieldwork
        at Allegany and Cattaraugus Seneca Reservations.
        Ms. in files of William C. Sturtevant.
Tanner, Adrian
1979   Bringing Home Animals: Religious Ideology and
        Mode of Production of the Mistassini Cree Hunters.
        New York: St. Martin's Press.

CHAPTER NINE

COMMENT

CALVIN MARTIN

PUT SIMPLY, *Keepers of the Game* is an effort to understand the world of humans and animals as that world was deeply shaken from the sixteenth through the early nineteenth centuries in eastern Canada. Though concentrating on Indian-animal relationships, the book also monitors the broader internal repercussions of European contact, particularly in the context of the fur trade and its sister institution, missionization. Anyone who has read the book can see for himself that it is in many respects inconclusive. My aim was to discern the thought-world, the cosmology, of these early historic hunter-gatherers as it reeled under the impact of Western influence; I tried to get into the minds of these people and see the changing world through their cultural prism. The end product was a structure, an explanation, that seemed to me to fit the disparate lines of evidence I invoked: contemporary European commentary, native oral testimony and literature, ethnographic analogy, biomedicine. It is a book of controlled imagination, well within the usual scholarly bounds. In the final analysis, a book of such a speculative nature either rings true or it does not. For me, not surprisingly, *Keepers of the Game* rings true. On this plane I like to think the book has made a substantial contribution to knowledge.

But the authors of the seven preceding essays are not concerned with the book on this plane. Their interest is the "war against animals" idea that I proposed as an explanation for the incipient fur trade in this part of the continent. Each of the foregoing authors has challenged my interpretation in one way or another, and with one exception I intend to leave it to the reader of my book to decide on the merits of their case versus mine.

I would like to comment on William Sturtevant's "Animals and Disease in Indian Belief," which I find especially interesting. Whereas the other six authors in this volume are adequately rebutted or their points sufficiently addressed in *Keepers*, Sturtevant's provocative point is not, and so deserves special consideration.

Sturtevant quotes A. I. Hallowell to the effect that animal bosses are always benevolent beings who "do not afflict human beings with illness. By and large, they are not characterized by any punishing role. Their attitude toward *anicinabek* [Ojibwa] is one of helpfulness. . . . It is true that if men do not treat game animals properly, the 'persons' who are their 'masters' will not allow these animals to be caught. But the human offenders are not afflicted with sickness on this account" (Hallowell 1963: 278–79). This seems straightforward enough, and, as Sturtevant points out, it does seem to contradict directly my claim that animals did indeed cause disease.

We continue reading Hallowell's article (which I quoted and discussed on p. 129 of *Keepers*), and we find that things begin to get muddled. For example: "While it is necessary, of course, for men to kill animals in order to live, what is wrong is to cause them unnecessary suffering. I believe that the disease sanction is applicable to the treatment of animals because cruelty to individual animals is offensive to the 'persons' who are their 'masters.' Thus, the breadth of the sanction against cruelty is as wide as it is deep in the Ojibwa ethos" (1963:286). (We can only guess what Hallowell meant by this final sentence.) So far, then, it has been established that the animal overlords are offended—could one say angered?—by indiscreet behavior toward game, which are now withdrawn from the guilty hunter (as punishment?). Somewhere in here a disease sanction is invoked: the offending hunter or his family or the hunting group may take sick as a result of his or their infraction. Where does the disease originate? Or, since the Saulteaux personalize things of this nature, we might more properly ask, *Who* sent the illness? Hallowell is misty on this point.

Self-discipline underlies the self-reliance that is required of the hunter. An illness which is thought to eventuate from the violation of moral obligations to "our grandfathers" [and this would include the game bosses] cannot be interpreted as stemming from their anger. *They* have done what they could for me; they have fulfilled their role. On my side, I must be able to accept obligations and fulfill them if I wish to reap the benefit of the help I have been offered by them. Among other things, self-discipline is necessary. The severity of the disease sanction in such cases is psychologically sound, if it is interpreted as a means of reinforcing motivations connected with self-discipline, for the Ojibwa are a people for whom life is fraught with objective hazards, which are inescapable. At the same time the sanction lends support, in principle, to moral responsibility for conduct in *all* interpersonal relations. Human beings *can* obtain vital help in meeting the hazards of life from other-than-human persons [such as game bosses] so long as they fulfill the obligation imposed by "our grandfathers." Knowing this, a sense of security is fostered. [1963:285]

What Hallowell appears to be saying is that an act or acts offensive to the spiritual gamekeepers may well result ("eventuate" is the word he uses) in disease to the guilty human party. What or who, exactly, is the source of the disease? "'Other-than-human persons' [such as game bosses] *may become involved in illness*, as well as human beings. The many sources to which it is possible to attribute illness, combined with its linkage with primary emotions, is one of the great advantages of such a sanction in relation to man's organized social existence" (1963: 264–65; my emphasis). And yet a dozen or so pages later he writes, as we saw above, "'Our grandfathers' [another term for the "other-than-human persons"] . . . do not afflict human beings with illness" (p. 278). And for an encore in contradictions: When disease "eventuates" from a violation of the human-animal code, "the northern Ojibwa . . . are among the people whose central values are reinforced by the belief that sickness is a penalty for bad conduct" (p. 266); whereas later on he declares, "By and large, they ["our grandfathers," the "other-than-human persons"] are not characterized by any punishing role" (p. 278).

In sum, on p. 264 it is granted that game bosses "may become involved in illness," whereas on p. 278 we are told they "do not afflict human beings with illness"; on p. 266 sickness mysteriously resulting from a hunting infraction is conceded to be a "penalty for bad conduct," but on p. 278 this, too, is evidently denied: the game bosses are not punitive. On p. 286 the game lords are offended by indiscreet hunting; on p. 285 they are not. It's a semantic madhouse.

Hallowell needs to be clarified. His claim that animals and animal bosses are thoroughly benevolent beings just does not square with ethnographic and indeed historic data on Canadian boreal zone hunter-gatherers. Animal beings in Subarctic cosmology are in fact capable of hostile, punitive behavior toward humankind, and punishment may take the form of disease. Frank Speck, writing of the Montagnais-Naskapi, was rather blunt about animals and animal overlords trafficking in disease: "The fatalities of life are represented in starvation, freezing, accident, and disease for which the animals, animal overlords, plant spirits, and demons of nature, and monsters are responsible. The individual has only to rely upon their benevolence for his welfare. His own soul is his medium of power in the struggle against their force" (1935:81). Diamond Jenness made a similar point about the Parry Island Ojibwa (actually Potawatomi): "Then again the animals may punish with sickness persons who speak ill of them, or show them disrespect by throwing their bones to the dogs" (1935:89). And Robert Ritzenthaler, who specialized in Chippewa health and disease, once remarked: "In my search through considerable literature dealing with the attitude of Indians toward disease, I was struck by a rather curious, but recurring phenomenon. Namely, that there is a tremendously widespread tendency among American Indians to associate animals with disease. Furthermore, . . . such associations are as prominent among agricultural tribes as among hunting tribes" (1953:243).

Curiously, Hallowell seems to know all of this and indeed to say as much. But, as Sturtevant observes, he also denies it. What he *may* be trying to say is that in Saulteaux society, yes, animal overlords dispense disease when human persons have contravened the hunting ethic but this chastening, like Jehovah's chastening in the Judeo-Christian tradition, is in truth a benevolent act—"the Lord chastens those whom he loves" sort of thing. An interpretation of this nature would tend to resolve what otherwise appear to be contradictions in Hallowell's essay.

In view of all the foregoing, Sturtevant's argument that "humans become afflicted (intransitively)" is ultimately not sustainable. Subarctic Indian disease ideology, including Hallowell's enigmatic rendition of it, has it that illness which results from disrespect to animals is indeed of animal origin—is exogenous, compliments of the game bosses. Sturtevant goes on: "According to Hallowell, then, the animals have behaved properly. If there is illness, the human must have failed somehow in interpersonal relations, not the animals. The problem is to discover what this human misbehavior may have been. . . . It is clear," he then concludes, "that in the Ojibwa view . . . it would make no sense whatsoever to take revenge on game animals for human illness." In general, it *is* true that an illness suspected of being sent by the game lords is taken as a sign of failure in human-animal relations, with the blame resting with the human partner in the transaction. Under ordinary circumstances the illness is interpreted as a righteous chastening by the animal beings whose aim is to restore cordial relations between the two, humans and animals—so Hallowell appears to be saying. It does not necessarily follow, however, that "it would make no sense whatsoever to take revenge on game animals for human illness." Animal bosses are a source of major disease; that, I think, has been sufficiently well established for the eastern Subarctic. Novel disease, catastrophic disease of the sort experienced in early historic and protohistoric times—epidemics attested in native folklore and described by these people in interviews with Europeans—may indeed have been construed as a massive dose of animal-originated contagion. I still find it conceivable that disease on this scale and of such destructive force was viewed by its human victims as an unwarranted, irregular, and horrifying assault on them by gamekeepers now turned seemingly hostile and treacherous. Or, as I phrased it in *Keepers*, "Is it not reasonable to assume that these people, who were seemingly accustomed to blaming offended wildlife for their sicknesses, would have blamed them as well for the new contagions?" (p. 146). This sentence might be recast to read, "Is it not reasonable to assume that these people, who seemingly considered animals to be the source of major disease, would have assigned the new contagions to them as well?" Sturtevant continues to quote me. "In an attempt to extricate himself from their morbid grip, the Indian sought to destroy his wildlife tormentors: he went on a war of revenge, a war which soon became transformed into the historic fur trade" (p. 146).

The "war against animals" idea. In his *Nouvelle Relation de la Gaspésie* (Paris, 1691) Father Chrestien Le Clercq, considered by the *Dictionary of Canadian Biography* to be an unimpeachable source on the Micmac, phrased the idea very elegantly. At the end of twelve years' labor in the vineyards of the Gaspé Peninsula he wrote that the Micmac, for whom the beaver still "have sense, and form a separate nation," "say they would cease to make war upon these animals if these would speak, howsoever little, in order that they might learn whether the Beavers are among their friends or their enemies" (in the original, ". . . qu'ils cesseroient de leur faire la guerre, s'ils parloient tant soit peu, pour leur apprendre s'ils sont de leurs amis, ou de leurs ennemis") (Le Clercq 1910:277, 421). It's an eerie statement, an astonishing and haunting revelation. Nor were the Micmac alone in this sentiment, as *Keepers of the Game* makes clear. It is still my belief that the "war upon these animals" was quite possibly triggered by the arrival of European disease, blamed, most unfortunately, on profoundly offended or treacherous wildlife spirits. Despite the seven preceding essays, I remain unreconstructed.

References Cited

Hallowell, A. Irving
　1963　Ojibwa World View and Disease. *In* Man's Image in
　　　　Medicine and Anthropology, ed. Iago Galdston, pp.
　　　　258–315. Institute of Social and Historical Medicine,
　　　　New York Academy of Medicine, Monograph 4.
　　　　New York: International Universities Press.
Jenness, Diamond
　1935　The Ojibwa Indians of Parry Island: Their Social and
　　　　Religious Life. Canada Department of Mines. Na-
　　　　tional Museum of Canada Bulletin No. 78. An-
　　　　thropological Series No. 17. Ottawa.
Le Clercq, Father Chrestien
　1910　New Relation of Gaspesia, with the Customs and
　　　　Religion of the Gaspesian Indians (1691). William F.
　　　　Ganong, trans. and ed. Toronto: The Champlain
　　　　Society.
Martin, Calvin
　1978　Keepers of the Game: Indian-Animal Relationships
　　　　and the Fur Trade. Berkeley: University of California
　　　　Press.
Ritzenthaler, Robert E.
　1953　Chippewa Preoccupation with Health: Change in a
　　　　Traditional Attitude Resulting from Modern Health
　　　　Problems. Bulletin of the Public Museum of the City
　　　　of Milwaukee 19 (December):175–257.
Speck, Frank G.
　1935　Naskapi: The Savage Hunters of the Labrador Penin-
　　　　sula. Norman: University of Oklahoma Press.

CONTRIBUTORS

CHARLES A. BISHOP is professor of anthropology at the State University of New York College, Oswego. He has conducted fieldwork among the Northern Ojibwa and the Six Nations Iroquois and has done extensive archival research. His publications include *The Northern Ojibwa and the Fur Trade: An Historical and Ecological Study*, "The Emergence of Hunting Territories among the Northern Ojibwa," "The Emergence of the Northern Ojibwa: Social and Economic Consequences," and "Northern Algonkian Cannibalism and Windigo Psychosis."

LYDIA T. BLACK is associate professor of anthropology at Providence College. Her doctoral dissertation, "Dogs, Bears, and Killer Whales: Analysis of the Nivkh Symbolic System," was concerned in part with conceptualizations of the relationships between humans and animals. She is the author of *History of the Atka District*, "Aleutians before 1867," and "Ivan Pan'kov: An Architect of Aleut Literacy" and the translator and editor of "The Konyag (The Inhabitants of the Island of Kodiak) by Iosef [Bolotov] (1794–1799) and by Gideon (1804–1807)."

CHARLES M. HUDSON, JR., is professor of anthropology at the University of Georgia. His research has been on the culture and history of Indians of the southeastern United States. He is author of *The Southeastern Indians*, *The Catawba Nation*, and numerous articles, and editor of *Four Centuries of Southern Indians* and *Black Drink*.

Contributors

SHEPARD KRECH III is associate professor of anthropology at George Mason University. He has conducted fieldwork among the Kutchin and has done extensive archival research on Northern Athapaskans. His publications, focusing mainly on ethnohistory and social organization, include "Disease, Starvation and Northern Athapaskan Social Organization," "The Nakotcho Kutchin: A Tenth Aboriginal Kutchin Band?" and "Northern Athapaskan Ethnology in the 1970s: A Critical Review."

CALVIN MARTIN is associate professor of history at Rutgers University. He is author of *Keepers of the Game: Indian-Animal Relationships and the Fur Trade*, "The War between Indians and Animals," "Wildlife Diseases as a Factor in Depopulation of the North American Indian," and "Ethnohistory: A Better Way to Write Indian History."

DEAN R. SNOW is professor of anthropology at the State University of New York, Albany. His publications on ethnohistory and archaeology include *Archaeology of North America, Native American Prehistory, Archaeology of New England*, and chapters on prehistory of the East Coast and on the Abenaki in Volume 15 (Northeast) of the *Handbook of North American Indians*.

WILLIAM C. STURTEVANT is curator of North American ethnology at the Smithsonian Institution and adjunct professor of anthropology at Johns Hopkins University. His ethnographic work includes fieldwork among the Seminole and the Seneca, and his research has focused on ethnohistory, ethnobotany and other aspects of ethnoscience. He is the general editor of the *Handbook of North American Indians* and the author of numerous publications, including "Anthropology, History, and Ethnohistory," and "Studies in Ethnoscience."

BRUCE G. TRIGGER is professor of anthropology at McGill University. He is the author of numerous articles and books, including *The Children of Aataentsic: A History of the Huron People to 1660*, *The Huron: Farmers of the North*, "Hochelaga: History and Ethnohistory," and "Iroquoian Matriliny" and is the editor of Volume 15 (Northeast) of the *Handbook of North American Indians*.

INDEX

Abenaki, 6, 23, 64–69; and epidemics, 65; fur trade, 65, 68–69; shamanism, 67–68; subsistence, 64
Adair, James, 161
Aleut, 7, 111–53; belief system, 116–17, 131–37; conceptualization of animals, 124–31; conversion to Christianity, 131–37; disease causation, 116, 132; and the fur trade, 117–24; population, 140; shamans, 117, subsistence, 115–16
Algonkians, 5, 21, 42–56; fur trade among, 46–51. *See also* Abenaki, Algonkin, Chippewa, Cree, Micmac, Montagnais, Naskapi, Nipissing, Odawa, Penobscot
Algonkin, 5, 21, 23, 26, 33
Animal Spirits. *See* Disease, Indian explanation of
Animals: bear, 89, 90, 94; beaver, 6, 16–17, 27–28, 35, 51, 68, 77, 79, 81, 85, 89–90, 94, 114, 160, 163, 165; caribou, 8, 55, 66, 79, 84–87, 89–92, 96; deer, 7, 159–60, 162–63, 165–67, 171; fox, 68, 90, 94, 115, 118, 123–25; frog, 92, 94; fur seal, 7, 115–16, 121, 124–26; groundhog, 94; hair seal, 115, 124, 126; lynx, 89, 91, 94; marmot, 90; marten, 77, 81, 85, 89, 91–92, 94; mink, 89, 92, 94; moose, 91, 93; mountain goat, 93; mountain sheep, 93; muskrat, 81, 94; otter (land), 89, 91, 92, 94; otter

(sea), 7, 114–31 passim, 142n; porcupine, 94; rabbit, 94; sea lion, 115, 124; weasel, 92; whale, 114–16, 123–24, 128–30; wolverine, 89, 91, 94. *See also* Disease, Indian explanation of; Indian-animal relationship; Overhunting
Animals, Indian conceptualization of. *See* Indian-animal relationship
Apalachee, 161, 163, 167
Apostatization. *See* Belief system, despiritualization
Arctic drainage lowlands Athapaskans, 85, 88. *See also* Beaver Indians, Chipewyan, Dogrib, Hare, Slavey, Yellowknife

Bear. *See* Animals, bear
Beaver. *See* Animals, beaver
Beaver Indians, 182
Belief system, Indian, 8, 18, 29–34, 43–45, 67–68, 82, 85–99 passim, 116–17, 124–37 passim, 159–61, 179–85, 192–96; compared to Russian Orthodoxy, 134–37; and conversion to Christianity, 131–37; and cultural elaboration, 45; and despiritualization, 4, 6, 17–18, 44–45; impact of Christian missionaries on, 18, 23, 28, 30–32, 41–42, 76, 164–67. *See also* Disease, Indian explanation of; Indian-animal relationship

203

Index

Biard, Pierre, 32
Black, Mary B., 185n
Black Death, 32

Caribou. *See* Animals, caribou
Carlson, Leonard, 5
Carrier, 48
Cherokee, 5, 159–62
Chipewyan, 5, 7, 76, 84–88, 96–99;
  and caribou, 84–87, 96; diseases
  among, 85–86; and the fur trade,
  85, 96; *inkonze* ("enabling knowl-
  edge"), 87–88
Chippewa, 194. *See also* Ojibwa
Cholera, 86. *See also* Epidemics
Clark, Annette McFadyen, 89
Conservation, 8, 18, 52–56, 87, 96;
  and caribou, 96; and ethnocen-
  trism, 8, 53, 96; of fur seals, 121;
  and Indians as ecologists, 13–14,
  141n; of sea otters, 120–21, 128.
  See also Overhunting
Coosa, 160, 161
Cree, 16, 18, 48–49, 84–85, 182
Cusabao, 166–67
Cusso, 166–68

Deer. *See* Animals, deer
DeLoria, Vine, Jr., 13
Denys, Nicolas, 25
Despiritualization. *See* Belief system,
  despiritualization
Diereville, Sieur de, 16
Disease, 3–4, 7, 17, 23, 29–31, 41, 45,
  75, 81–85, 115–16, 140–41n,
  179–80, 194–96; and curing rituals,
  29–31; early spread of, 17, 42; etiology, 6, 99, 160; mortality in
  epidemic, 23–24, 81–82, 90, 161;
  starvation and, 23, 29; and whites,
  97. *See also* Disease, Indian explanation of; Epidemics; Taboo violation
Disease, epidemic. *See* Epidemics
Disease, Indian explanation of: Ae-
  taentsic, 6, 29; animal spirits, 4,
  17–18, 29, 42, 89–90, 92–96,
  130–31, 159–62, 179–80, 192–96;

human carriers, 18, 85–86, 91; *inkonze*, 88; moral transgression,
  116–17, 131–32, 160–62, 180–85
  passim; omens, 90; shamans, 8,
  67–68, 82, 89–90, 92–93; sorcery, 6,
  7, 33–34, 82–84, 86–88, 91–99, 160;
  spirit loss, 82; witchcraft, 32–34,
  36, 92, 160. *See also* Disease; Epidemics; Taboo violation
Dogrib, 87–88, 91–92
Dysentery, 85. *See also* Epidemics

Epidemics, 3–4, 6, 8, 17, 29, 32–33,
  36, 42, 45, 65, 75, 95–96, 99, 112,
  158–59, 162, 165, 179, 195–96;
  among Aleuts, 115, 140–41n;
  among Arctic Drainage Lowlands
  Athapaskans, 85; among Huron, 6,
  22–24, 32–34; among Koyukon, 90;
  among Kutchin, 7, 81–82; among
  Northeastern Indians, 17, 22–24;
  among Southeastern Indians, 7,
  161–62. *See also* Cholera; Disease;
  Disease, Indian explanation of;
  Dysentery; Influenza; Measles;
  Plague; Pleurisy; Scarlet fever;
  Smallpox; Tularemia
Eskimo (Inuit), 76–80, 94, 97, 136
Ethnohistory, 3, 6, 8, 9, 62, 65, 78, 95,
  99; and American Society for Ethnohistory, 9, 61; ethnohistorical
  methodology in, 5, 41–43, 51,
  62–63, 70, 88–91, 99. *See also* Fur
  trade explanations, Historiography
Evans-Pritchard, E. E., 158, 171
Ewers, John, 5

Family hunting territory, 54; and con-
  servation, 27–28, 43–44
Feast of the Dead, 25, 45, 47
Feit, Harvey, 43
Fischer, David, 61
Fox. *See* Animals, fox
Frog. *See* Animals, frog
Fur-bearers. *See* Animals
Fur seal. *See* Animals, fur seal
Fur trade, 3, 5, 9, 14, 24–28, 35–36,

204

46–56, 65–70, 76–81, 85, 99–100, 114, 117–24, 162–63; dependency, 24, 35–36, 51; effect on maize horticulture, 65; as gift exchange, 69; and ritual elaboration, 25–26, 47; technological impact of, 50–51. *See also* Conservation; Fur trade, Indian motivations in; Fur trade explanations; Overhunting

Fur trade explanations, 3, 7, 8, 36, 45; and formal economic theory, 3, 47–49, 62, 173n; as idealist, 7, 36; and impressment of Aleuts, 118, 120; and market economy, 137; as materialist, 7–8, 14, 36, 50, 69–70, 81, 99–100, 137–38; and modern world system, 7, 166–72 passim; role of ideology in, 6, 41, 63–70, 112–14, 170–72; and substantive-formalist debate, 62; and Western economic man, 46, 179. *See also* Disease, Indian explanation of; Fur trade, Indian motivations in

Fur trade, Indian motivations in: desire for European trade goods, 3, 14, 24–25, 47, 77–81; desire for prestige, 47, 50, 78–79; leisure, 24–25, 48; middlemen profits, 26, 48–49, 80–81, 96; military advantages, 24–25, 78–79; political advantages, 169; power through intoxication, 150; retaliation against animals for disease, 4, 8, 18, 46, 179, 196; security, 24–25; survival, 168. *See also* Fur trade; Fur trade explanations

Geertz, Clifford, 112
Graymont, Barbara, 4
Groundhog. *See* Animals, groundhog

Hair Seal. *See* Animals, hair seal
Hallowell, A. Irving, 8, 43, 181–84, 192–95
Han, 83, 92–93, 97
Hare (Indians), 91
Harris, Marvin, 21, 53

Hearne, Samuel, 86–87, 96, 98–99
Henry, Alexander, 8, 16
Historiography, 5, 21, 51, 61–63, 70, 158–59, 170–72, 180–91; and explanation in anthropology and history, 172, 184–85; and ethnocentrism, 179. *See also* Ethnohistory; Fur trade explanations
Hooper, Calvin L., 122–23
Horticulturalists, 5, 158–59. *See also* Huron, Southeastern Indians
Hudson's Bay Company, 69, 76–100 passim
Hunter-gatherers. *See* Northern Athapaskans; Algonkians
Huron, 5, 21–36; Feast of the Dead, 25–26; fur trade, 24–26, 35–36; epidemic diseases among, 22–24; overkill of beaver, 27–28; shamanism and ritual, 29–32
Hutchison, W. H., 13–14

Indian-animal relationship, 4, 42, 44–45, 116, 129–31, 159–60, 179–85 passim, 192–96 passim; and animals as persons, 15; and animals as transformed humans, 116, 125, 26; and guardian spirit, 87–88, 90–91; as hostile, 16–18, 196; and respect of animals, 15, 82, 84, 86–87, 89, 91–94. *See also* Belief system
Influenza, 17, 23. *See also* Epidemics
Iroquois, 22, 23, 25, 27, 28, 171, 179

Jaenan, Cornelius, 5
Jenness, Diamond, 194
Jennings, Francis, 5
Jetté, Julius, 89–91

Kaska, 92, 97, 100
Koyukon, 5, 7, 76, 84, 99; explanations of disease, 88–91
Kutchin, 7, 75–84, 95, 97, 99–100; and diseases, 81–82; explanations of disease, 82–84; and the fur trade, 76–81, 99–100

Index

LeClercq, Chrestien, 16, 196
LeJeune, Paul, 27
Lévi-Strauss, Claude, 62, 181
Lévy-Bruhl, Lucien, 157–58
Lower Creek, 169–70
Lynx. *See* Animals, lynx

McClellan, Catharine, 93–94
Mackenzie, Alexander, 81
Man-animal relationship. *See* Indian-animal relationship
Marmot. *See* Animals, marmot
Marsh, Gordon H., 136
Marten. *See* Animals, marten
Martin, Calvin, 3–9, 13–18, 21, 24–26, 29, 31–32, 35–36, 41–56 passim, 61–70 passim, 75, 84, 88–89, 95–96, 99, 111–13, 131–32, 158–65 passim, 170–72, 179–85, 191–96
Marx, Karl, 171
Matonabbee, 96, 98–99
Matrilocality, 53
Measles, 23, 85. *See also* Epidemics
Methodology. *See* Ethnohistory, ethnohistorical methodology in; Historiography
Micmac, 4, 5, 16, 32, 196
Midewiwin, 45
Mink. *See* Animals, mink
Mohawk, 23, 24
Momaday, N. Scott, 13
Montagnais, 5, 21, 24, 25, 26, 27–28, 33, 194
Moorehead complex, 66
Moose. *See* Animals, moose
Moral transgression. *See* Disease, Indian explanation of
Mountain goat. *See* Animals, mountain goat
Mountain sheep. *See* Animals, mountain sheep
Murray, Alexander Hunter, 80, 83
Muskrat. *See* Animals, muskrats

Naskapi, 182, 194
Nipissing, 21, 26, 33

Northeastern Indians, 6, 41–57, 159. *See also* Algonkians
Northern Athapaskans, 5, 7, 75–108. *See also* Beaver Indians, Carrier, Chipewyan, Dogrib, Han, Hare, Kaska, Koyukon, Kutchin, Slavey, Southern Tutchone, Yellowknife
North West Company, 76–77, 86

Odawa, 21, 26
Ojibwa, 5, 8, 16, 18, 45, 51, 84, 181–84, 192–95; belief system, 182–84; disease theory, 182–84, 192–95
Ortega y Gasset, José, 112
Otter, land. *See* Animals, otter (land)
Otter, sea. *See* Animals, otter (sea)
Overhunting, 3, 4, 14, 52–56, 79; of beaver, 27–28, 79; of deer, 159, 162–63, 167; of fur seals, 121; and market economy, 121, 137; and Pleistocene extinctions, 54; role of non-natives in, 68, 118–23, 138–39; of sea-otters, 118–22, 138–39; and use of firearms, 111, 122, 138–39
Overkill. *See* Overhunting

Penobscot, 69, 182
Plague, 17, 115. *See also* Epidemics
Pleistocene extinctions. *See* Overhunting, and Pleistocene extinctions
Pleurisy, 91. *See also* Epidemics
Porcupine. *See* Animals, porcupine

Rabbit. *See* Animals, rabbit
Ray, Arthur J., 49
Rich, E. E., 69
Ritzenthaler, Robert, 194
Russian American Company, 78, 117, 119–20; and role of creoles, 120

Sagard, Gabriel, 27
Scarlet fever, 82. *See also* Epidemics
Sea lion. *See* Animals, sea lion
Seminole, 179

Shamanism. *See* Disease, Indian explanation of
Shelikov, Grigorii, 119
Slaves, 162–63, 166–67
Slavey, 87–88, 92
Smallpox, 17, 23, 86, 91, 93, 115. *See also* Epidemics
Smith, Adam, 47
Smith, James G. E., 87
Sorcery. *See* Disease, Indian explanation of
Southeastern Indians, 7, 157–72, 179; deerskin and slave trade among, 162–63; disease theory, 160–62; epidemics among, 160–62; missions among, 163–65; in a modern world economic system, 166–72; and relationship to animals, 159–62. *See also* Apalachee, Cherokee, Cusaboa, Cusso, Lower Creek, Stono, Upper Creek, Westoes
Southern Tutchone, 93–94, 97
Speck, Frank G., 43, 70, 181, 182
Starvation. *See* Disease, starvation and
Stono, 168
Strickland, Rennard, 13
Sturtevant, William C., 191
Sullivan, Robert J., 84, 88–90
Susquehannock, 23
Swanson, Henry, 123

Taboo violation, 4, 8, 82, 86–94 passim, 179–80, 191–96 passim; and bad luck, 87; and blame of oneself, 8, 132, 180; and death, 89–91, 92, 94–95; and link between specific species and specific illnesses, 96, 179; and scarcity of or access to animals, 8, 86, 89–90, 93–94, 192; and sickness, 4, 89–91, 92, 94–95, 194; and specific misfortune, 93–94; specific action as, 86–94. *See also* Disease, Indian explanation of
Tanner, Adrian, 43, 131
Thomas, Keith, 171
Thompson, David, 8, 16
Tularemia, 115. *See also* Epidemics

Upper Creek, 165, 169

Veniaminov, Ioann, 116, 127, 129, 134

Wallerstein, Immanuel, 167
Weasel. *See* Animals, weasel
Wenroronon, 23
Westoes, 166, 168, 173
Whale. *See* Animals, whale
Witchcraft. *See* Disease, Indian explanation of
Wolverine. *See* Animals, wolverine

XY Company, 76–77

Yellowknife, 87